THE MOST IMPORTANT SPACE IN THE CHURCH

THE MOST IMPORTANT SPACE IN THE CHURCH

The Nursery

Rita Hays

DISCIPLESHIP RESOURCES

P O BOX 340003 • NASHVILLE, TN 37203-0003
www.discipleshipresources.org

ISBN 978-0-88177-568-6
Library of Congress Control Number 2009925607

To the memory of my mother Ruth Brannon Barlow
Caregiver & Nurturer

As a teacher she touched the lives of countless young people,
providing them with lessons in business practices and in life.

As a mother she taught me the lessons of courage, faith,
and fortitude and the value of education.

CONTENTS

INTRODUCTION

There is a space in your church called the nursery. Often tucked away in the remote corners of your church building, few realize its power to transform the life of your congregation. Inside its walls can be heard the sounds of babies crying, nursery workers singing, and toddlers laughing. Yet if that is all you hear when you walk by your church nursery, you need to stop and listen more carefully. There are lessons being taught and lessons being learned.

Ask your church members to tell you what space in the church they consider the most important. No doubt, you will receive a myriad of responses. Some persons will be adamant that the **sanctuary** has to be the most valuable space in the church. In the sanctuary, we are welcomed to the Lord's Table, we witness the baptism of God's children, and our souls are nourished by sermons, Scripture readings, music, and liturgy.

Other individuals will be certain that the **gathering space** must be considered the most important space. The gathering area is often the space inside the church building in which visitors will first arrive, seeking information about the church and waiting for a welcome from the congregation.

You will discover that some church members will rank as their top selections your **fellowship hall** along with the **church kitchen**. Individuals will point out to you that meals in both Jewish and Christian traditions were pivotal occasions for sharing. Social events, wedding receptions, Wednesday night dinners, meals provided for those in need in the community, and a meal prepared for a family after a funeral are all marks of the congregation that understands its calling to live together as the family of God.

Advocates for Christian education might vote for the **Sunday school classrooms** as the most vital space in the church. They will tell you that these spaces contain classes for all ages and provide areas where faith formation, Bible study, nurture, fellowship, and outreach take place on a consistent basis.

Rarely does anyone in your congregation name the **nursery** as the most important space in the church. It never enters some of your church members' minds that your nursery might even make the top ten list in importance, let alone be considered first. "Out of sight, out of mind," might be representative of the thoughts and feelings some of your members express toward the nursery. This book makes the argument, though, that the nursery is not only the most important space in the church, but that the nursery space holds lessons that the entire church needs to learn!

Our journey of faith begins at birth. The care that children receive in your church nursery will have an impact on their faith formation throughout their lives. From the church nursery, your congregation can learn lessons about the effective ways to nurture, the practical ways to encourage and develop faith, the grace-filled ways to practice hospitality, and the loving ways to relate to one another as brothers and sisters in Christ.

Are we willing to see, listen, and apply the lessons that our nursery children are learning? Are we ready to learn, recognizing that we are children of God, hungry and needing to be fed like our nursery children? We will have to be open, honest, and humble in our way of thinking and learning in order to grasp these lessons.

Many books have been written on the ways to help your nursery become a safe and excellent environment. These books have included lists of nursery supplies, ideas for furnishing the nursery, policies and guidelines, and requirements for childcare workers and volunteers. This book will move us beyond these issues to affirm the ways the nursery can model for the entire congregation some of the church's most important tasks.

All of our church spaces hold the potential as places where all of God's children can grow in grace. For this reason, all of our church spaces can be seen as sacred. Using the church nursery as our model, we move out to transform other spaces of the church into holy, sacred places.

If you do not see that picture of grace at work in your church nursery, then do all in your power as a church leader to make changes. There is too much at stake for you not to speak up and take action. Do it for the sake of the each infant God has entrusted to your care. Do it for the sake of each child God has given you the responsibility to nurture in the faith. Do it for the sake of the future generations who will begin their faith journey in your church nursery. Do it, because without a strong nursery foundation, your congregation will never be as grounded as it can become. Do it, knowing that an excellent nursery will make the greatest difference in the life of your church. Share with others the impact the nursery can have on the entire congregation. There are lessons the nursery can and should teach your church. Is your church ready and willing to learn?

Rita B. Hays
Nashville, Tennessee

Chapter One

I AM A CHILD OF GOD

A Virtual Reality Tour of Spaces in the Church

The uprooted Garcia family faces an uncertain future. Anthony, Margo, their three children, one dog, and two cats are moving cross-country! Besides leaving behind the familiar comforts of their community, friends, school, church, and family, they are challenged with finding a new home before school begins in two months. To save time, Anthony and Margo search the housing market through their home computer. By means of virtual tours, they look at house after house, room by room. Thus they are able to narrow their list down to a few homes to view that the Garcia family believes are worth the lengthy travel to view in person.

When it comes time to "shop" for a new congregation to call "home", the Garcia family wishes they could take a virtual tour of the churches in the area. Suppose your church were on the virtual "church shopping" tour of the Garcia family. Would the spaces in your church be so appealing and inviting that the Garcia family would want to visit your church building in person?

Let's take a virtual reality tour of a church with the Garcia family. We begin in the sanctuary during a morning worship service. Scanning the room, the Garcia family notices worshipers from different generations interacting with one another. Older adults share hugs with younger children. Middle age adults greet youth and reach out to hold infants. Visitors are welcomed by greeters and introduced to church members who invite them to sit with them. Visiting children are offered a worship bag and given information about Children's Church. The pastors mingle through-out the congregation, greeting parishioners and especially visitors. Scripture readings, the liturgy, and the music blend together with the theme of the pastor's sermon. Youth play a role in the service, one as a Scripture reader and one as an usher. The meaning of the church season and the liturgical color of the paraments are explained by the lay liturgist. Children serve as acolytes. The congregation enthusiastically vows to support a baby and his family as he receives the sacrament of infant baptism during the worship service. The Children's Chat contains vocabulary and a message relevant to the children. As the children leave the sanctuary for Children's Church, the Garcia family notices that the teachers for the day are a youth, an older adult man, and a younger adult woman. After the worship service is concluded, the pastors and some lay members gather in the narthex to greet visitors and offer them a welcome bag containing information about the church. The Garcia family comes away from their tour of the sanctuary convinced that in this congregation all ages are respected, loved, and valued as children of God. Can the same be said of the experience of worshipers in your sanctuary?

Just outside of the sanctuary the Garcias discover a large gathering area. People excitingly congregate in this area after the service. Some take time to stop and talk, while others speak or wave to friends while scurrying to their Sunday school class. Many stop by a table containing baked goods for sale by the youth, knowing the proceeds are designated for a mission project. Other individuals sign up for the Wednesday night meal. A beautiful glass case on a prominent wall contains items detailing the history of the church, including a plaque commemorating the twenty-five year anniversary of the church Boy Scout troop. Pictures on the walls near the gathering area show off framed photographs of pastors who have served the congregation.

As the Garcia family leaves the gathering area, they go down the halls toward the Sunday school classes. When they arrive at the first adult class, comprised of senior adults, what they initially notice is the way everyone is hugging and shaking hands with one another. They watch as the teacher escorts a visitor around the room and introduces her to regular members. The room's furnishings are chairs that appear to be comfortable for senior adults, a lectern for the teacher, an erase board, Bibles, religious paintings, and curtains. From the neat appearance of the room, one can tell that this class cares very much about the upkeep of their classroom and takes pride in keeping it tidy. Further down the hall, the Garcias observe other adult classes. One class, comprised of middle aged adults, talks with enthusiasm of their upcoming mission project. The women's class seriously engages in study of a Bible passage. The men's class chats about the weekend football games before beginning class with a prayer. A class of young adults discusses parenting issues and laughs at the antics of a class member's child. A class of newly married adults makes preparations to provide meals for a family with a newborn baby.

Since the Garcias have a youth in the family, they are very interested to get to the space occupied by the teenagers in the church. Traveling downstairs, they arrive at the youth area. The older teenagers are engaged in a game that goes along with their interactive Bible lesson. The room is filled with couches and posters of popular Christian music bands. Going into the next room, there is a ping-pong table, a television, a soft drink machine, and some video game systems. Jake Garcia is particularly excited when he views this room in virtual reality. He is reminded of the church youth room he is leaving behind and knows right away that he would enjoy this room very much. The Garcia family is glad to see that the younger teens have been given their own classroom, separate from the older youth. Sofas and beanbags are scattered around the room and colorful posters decorate the walls. Several of the youth are acting out a skit while others watch and giggle. The teacher gives the actors "high-fives" when they finish their skit.

Maggie Garcia, a third grader, waits patiently until the time they arrive at the children's area of the church. "Finally," she thinks, as she surveys the rooms for the children. All of the classrooms are brightly decorated with a fresh coat of paint and inspirational posters. The furniture in each classroom is designed for the age and physical characteristics of preschool and elementary children. Maggie joins in as the third grade class recites the Bible verse for the day. She smiles when she sees the teacher calling the students by name and praising them for their work.

The Garcias leave their tour of the classrooms assured that in this church Sunday school is a place where each generation of learners are valued as children of God. Can the same be said of what happens in the space you use in your church for Sunday school, nurture, and faith formation?

Leaving the Sunday school classroom spaces, the Garcias decide they need a break from their virtual tour. Having been regular participants in the Wednesday night programs of their previous congregation, they look forward to returning to their virtual tour on a Wednesday evening.

When Wednesday night arrives, they find themselves (virtually) in the kitchen, where individuals scurry around the kitchen, putting food on plates to be served for the evening's meal. Persons begin to line up outside the fellowship hall doors and, after a prayer of blessing, they hungrily grab their plates and carry them to the tables set up all around the fellowship hall. One of the older women in the church quickly hurries to sit with her adopted granddaughter. An "empty-nester" holds an infant so the baby's mother can fix her own plate and help her older child to the table. Soon a group of twelve men arrive at the church and are greeted by several members. Some of the church members leave the tables where they are sitting and integrate themselves among these guests, then invite these men to sit down with them at their tables. These are homeless men in the community, beneficiaries of an outreach ministry of the church called "Room in the Inn." Soon, with filled stomachs, the Wednesday night crowd disperses to the many activities the church offers. The homeless men go downstairs to prepare to shower, watch a movie, and get ready for sleep. The pastor invites adults to a Bible study, while other adults relax around the tables in the fellowship hall and participate in "table talks" where they discuss current issues. They watch the older children go to hand bells and the younger children to choir. Soon the order will be reversed. For those children who do not wish to participate in the music program, several adult volunteers lead children in mission projects.

The Garcia family likes what they are seeing and hearing. They experience the pleasure of brothers and sisters in Christ coming together for faith formation, nurture, and hospitality. They encounter intergenerational sharing. They come away from their virtual reality tour this Wednesday night convinced that this is a congregation that knows how to be the family of God. Can the same be said of the spaces you use on Wednesday night in your church?

The following Sunday the Garcia family decides to take one last virtual reality tour of this church. So far, they have been very impressed with their experience. When they previously toured the gathering area, a poster advertising the upcoming Blessing of the Animals captivated Anthony Garcia, as he has never heard of such an event. As a family of animal lovers, they decided to attend. They arrive on the church lawn just in time to view a menagerie of God's creatures. Attending the blessing are many dogs and cats, one turtle, two hamsters, one guinea pig, and a horse. They wish their own dog Tessa and cats Amy and Bob could be present. They need a blessing, given that they will soon be uprooted from their creature comforts!

Scanning the church grounds, they discover a beautiful prayer garden with stone benches. This garden resulted from the Eagle Scout project of a church youth. In addition to the garden, all of the church grounds are well kept. Anthony Garcia remarks on the church sign that contains a message welcoming the community to the Blessing of the Animals service, reinforcing his belief that this church cares about the community as well as its own members. Mr. Garcia also is pleased to see several handicap accessible parking spaces and visitor parking spaces. Margo Garcia's eyes are drawn to the church playground because the Garcia family has a nursery age infant. Margo checks out the playground equipment and the ground cover for safety issues. She was active on the nursery committee and Parent's Day Out committee at their previous congregation. Satisfied that the playground passes her stringent inspection, she would have no hesitation letting her infant son play there when he is old enough.

Does it seem strange to you that the Garcia family would take so much time to tour the church grounds of this church? Not really, if we consider all that might take place on the lawns of our church. The Blessings of the Animals service, the church's annual Easter egg hunt, the fall Trunk or Treat/Carnival are all events held on the church lawn and are community events. Prayers recited in the prayer garden have strengthened the believer's faith. Never underestimate the power of the church grounds to become spaces of hospitality, intergenerational sharing, faith formation, and nurture. Can the same be said of the space outside your church?

The Garcia family's virtual tour is not over, however. There is still one space left to explore. Situated at the back of the education wing, on the first floor of the church building are two rooms. What rooms are they? You guessed it: the church nursery! Why have Anthony and Margo Garcia chosen to wait and view these rooms last? If they decide to make this congregation their church home, then their infant son, Dominic, will occupy the infant nursery room each Sunday, each Wednesday, and as a part of the Parent's Day Out program of the church. So, would not it have made sense for Anthony and Margo to rush to view the nursery space right away on their virtual tour?

Anthony and Margo Garcia value the nursery care that their children have received so much that they would never leave Dominic in a church nursery that did not meet the standards they are accustomed to in their previous congregation. They planned all along, on their virtual church tour, to save the nursery to the end. They will study this space in great detail because they know the impact of excellent church nursery care on their children Jake and Maggie. They want to same care for infant Dominic.

Anthony and Margo recall what it was like when Margo was pregnant with Jake. Their church family reached out to them before Jake was even born. They were invited to take a tour of the church nursery, meet the nursery caregivers, and take part in a parenting class for new parents. When Jake was born, their Sunday school class showered them with meals and their congregation recognized and celebrated Jake's birth. How well they remember the first day they arrived at the doors of the church nursery with their newborn son and handed him to the nursery caregiver. She lovingly called him by name, greeted his parents, and provided them with information about the nursery. Thus began Jake's positive nursery experiences. He was fed, diapered, and rocked in a cheerful, comfortable, clean environment. The nursery room was equipped with toys and supplies adequate to meet his growing needs. He was sung Bible songs, told Bible stories, and taught about the love of God by several generations of believers who were his nursery caregivers. Maggie, their third grader, had a similar experience in the church nursery. Anthony and Margo look back and realize these children began their faith journey in the church nursery. When Dominic was born, the Garcia family once again experienced the support of their church family, particularly the nursery staff. These caregivers understood that the church nursery was much more than a space for babysitting; it was a place for faith formation and nurture.

Indelibly inked in Anthony and Margo's memories are the occasions when their children were baptized. Anthony and Margo took seriously the promises they took at the baptism of their children. They are thankful that the congregation upheld their vows to nurture the Garcia children in the Christian faith. Adopted grandparents, Sunday school teachers, Vacation Bible School volunteers, mentors, and friends continued the work of nurture and faith formation that began with nursery caregivers.

When Jake was in sixth grade, he decided he was ready for the confirmation class. On the day of his confirmation, his parents were powerfully reminded of his baptism. Jake took his own vows at his confirmation, confirming the vows taken on his behalf at his baptism. His church family witnessed his confirmation as a testimony to their own pledge made at Jake's baptism. The experience of grace at Jake's baptism extended to the experience of grace in the church nursery, and carried on into his faith journey as a child and youth.

Lessons in faith formation, nurture, grace, baptismal vows, and intergenerational sharing—lessons first learned in the nursery—are powerful lessons for *all* of God's children. Regardless of our ages, we never stop growing and we never stop needing to be fed by our Parent God. We never get too old or too big to be rocked in the arms of a loving God. When our rebellious nature and selfish pride take over, we can all use the discipline of our Caregiver. As a child of God, we never outgrow the need to be pampered. All of our lives, we remain hungry children, constantly in need of God's grace. Like infants learning to walk, we take tottering steps of faith. We sometimes stumble, but God comes to take our hands and lead us in the right direction. Like nursery children, our lessons of faith and trust are learned and reinforced daily by our relationship with others and our Creator.

What will the Garcia family learn from their virtual tour of the most important space in the church? We will never know because we must leave the Garcia family to complete their virtual church tour without us tagging along. We have some tours of our own to make, do we not? We are off to examine the spaces of our churches, starting with the most important space, the church nursery.

Chapter Two

I See You, I See God

Faith Formation in the Nursery & Church

A baby wakes up from her nap, hungry and with a wet diaper. Desiring to have her needs met, she cries out. Soon her mother and father enter the nursery room. They begin to care for their newborn, lovingly and tenderly. The father changes the baby's diaper, talking comforting "baby talk" to his infant daughter. The mother then takes the baby in her arms and rocks and feeds her child. The baby turns her head to meet the eyes of a loving mother and father. The journey of faith has begun for this child.

Caring parents are meeting the child's basic needs; thus, this child is learning to trust. She senses that her parents are dependable caregivers. During the first years of an infant's life, babies develop by negotiating between feelings of trust and mistrust. Loving, dependable parents meet the needs of the child. As this caring pattern is repeated time after time, the child learns to trust his or her parents. Faith grows as the child learns to trust. By association, the child senses that God can be trusted. However, if the child's needs are neglected in infancy, the child may come to sense that God cannot be trusted.[1]

This mutual bond of trust and loyalty seen in the interaction of this baby with her parents is vitally important when we consider faith formation. What happens in the family is essential for faith development. Faith grows primarily in relationship with others. As the baby moves beyond the family circle, others will care for the child's needs, and these caregivers will be important contributors to the child's faith development.

In the early weeks of life, babies spend many hours in the arms of their parents or other significant adults. The baby is often face to face with these persons. As the babies look into the eyes of their caregivers, they see in these eyes a reflection of how they are valued. They will view themselves in the manner in which those who care for them see the infants. In other words, in the eyes of their caregivers, they are able to see a picture of who they are in relationship to others. If the caregiver has eyes that reflect deep love and appreciation for the baby, the infant will see himself or herself as a person that is lovable and pleasing. Self-esteem is being built. If the eyes of the parents or caregivers are unresponsive or uncaring, the baby does not experience self-worth and feels ignored and rejected. As children create their early images of God, children will transfer what they have seen in the significant adults in their lives. They see themselves in the eyes of God in the same way they are viewed by others.[2]

Let's go a step further into the life of the baby mentioned at the beginning of this chapter. Suppose the parents take an active part in the life of a faith congregation. On Sunday morning, the regular routine of these parents is to arrive at this congregation with their infant daughter and head toward the nursery. Imagine in your mind the best scenario of the care this child and her parents will receive from their church nursery caregivers. They are greeted at the nursery door by the familiar face of the nursery worker who immediately calls the baby by name and welcomes her into loving arms. While the parents attend their Sunday school class and the worship service, this dependable paid nursery worker and her volunteers care for the child in a clean, cheerful environment. The caregivers rock the child, sing to the child, talk to the child, feed the child, and look into the eyes of the child with love and compassion. This infant has a good experience in the church nursery. She and her parents are blessed to belong to a church that makes the nursery a priority and a congregation whose leaders understand the importance of the nursery in shaping, along with parents and others, the faith formation of the infant.

Children begin to form their image of God as infants. Infants build their image of God from their experiences with families, friends, or at church. Our church nurseries are one of the most significant places for children to begin their faith formation. Babies should experience the church nursery as a place of trust and comfort. They need a familiar face to greet them from week to week. There must be enough volunteers to meet the babies' needs in a prompt manner. The church nursery ought to be a place of love and care, an extension of the love and care God shows for each of us as children of God.

Remember that trust and faith are bound together for the infant. If the baby does not experience the significant people in his or her world responding to his or her basic needs and doing so in a prompt, caring manner, then can the baby trust God as one who responds to his or her needs? In other words, if the child cannot trust these important people, then the child has difficulty believing in God as One who can be trusted. While parents and family are the most significant people in an infant's world, others in the congregation, especially nursery caregivers, have a critical role to play in faith formation for infants.

Why are church nurseries so important? We have already mentioned the significance of the home for early faith formation, yet the nursery will also be one of the first places that an infant may experience the love and grace of God. The church nursery is a place where faith formation will be instilled in the child week after week through the pleasant experiences of having needs met. The nursery is a place where caregivers begin to talk about God and sing about God as they care for the infant's needs. Through soothing words and lullabies sung about God's love, the child begins to hear about a God who is like a Parent. God cares for the child like the parents and nursery workers. As the nursery worker rocks the child, looks into the child's eyes, and calls the child by name, the infant grows in self-esteem. The infant begins to feel that he or she is a person of worth in God's eyes just as he or she is in the eyes of the nursery caregiver.

The task of the church and the Christian family is to instruct and lead the child in the ways of the Lord. Faith development for the infant begins in the home, but is reinforced each week by the church nursery. Parents bring their children to church because they want to see them grow in the faith. Church nurseries must view themselves as much more than places to babysit children while their parents are busy with church activities. Church nurseries are places where, along with the home, faith formation can be shaped and nurtured.

Faith formation begins the moment a child is born. Children come to the church nursery as spiritual beings. Churches must recognize this and instruct and prepare caregivers for the role they will play in spiritual formation with the nursery children. They must help the nursery workers understand that meeting the needs of the infants in a loving, affirming manner forms the basis of positive faith formation for babies.

The needs of infants are largely physical. It is important that a loving nursery caregiver meet the child's physical needs. These individuals have the responsibility of helping the infant form his or her first and most lasting impression of the place called church. Long before the baby knows anything about what is taught, he or she will know how he or she feels. If a child learns from his earliest days in the church nursery that he or she can trust others to meet his or her physical needs, then the child will know that God will meet his or her spiritual needs.

It is vitally important to communicate to the nursery workers that they are teaching love and trust to the child through their attitude and actions. The baby will respond positively to a quiet, calm, and unhurried atmosphere in which he or she feels secure and comfortable. Those who work with children in the nursery must be calm and secure in what they are doing in order to convey and transmit their feelings to the children. Remember that the sense of sight, taste, smell, and hearing are very alive in the newborn. Newborns learn through the senses. Take for example the sense of touch. Newborns recognize persons by the way they are handled. As a nursery worker changes a child's diaper or rocks that child, the baby's attitude can go from one of distress to comfort.

The same is true with the sense of smell and taste. Nursery workers who feed the child in a calm, pleasant mood convey a sense of trust and peace to the child. Feeding, changing, and holding give comfort. These feelings of comfort are associated with the people who care for the baby. If these pleasant experiences are occurring at the church nursery, then, in the infant's mind, the church nursery must be a happy, good, safe place where needs are met. As the child hears and learns about God in the church nursery the child develops faith in a God that is good and a God who provides a safe place.

Biblical Passages Offer Support

Scriptures in the Bible that bring to light the dignity and worth of children in the covenant community, and especially passages from the ministry and teachings of Jesus, will undergird the work and ministry of faith formation in the nursery. These Scriptures should be explained and interpreted for nursery workers, parents, and the congregation. Congregations sometimes find it difficult to understand theories of faith formation, but they are especially open to biblical passages that affirm the importance of children. Most church members have given little thought to the idea that babies begin their journey of faith formation at birth. Most desire to see the nursery as a well-kept place where children are loved and their basic needs are met, but beyond that, they have failed to realize the role of the church nursery in the area of faith formation.

Begin your teaching about the importance of faith formation for infants with biblical passages on the importance of children in the faith community. This is a starting point that can lead to further conversations and teaching about faith formation for infants. You will also discover that the congregation will begin to understand the importance of the church nursery as a place for helping infants on their faith journey when they have a better understanding of the biblical picture of children as a blessing.

Old Testament Passages

In the book of Genesis, God offers a blessing to Adam and Eve and children are included in the blessing. After God creates man and woman as recorded in Genesis 1, God blesses Adam and Eve and tells them to be fruitful and multiply, so that the blessing falls not just upon them, but also upon their future children. When God calls Abraham into a covenant relationship, God promises to make his descendants as great as the stars in the heavens. Obviously, children have to be present in order to make this happen! The psalmist declares that women are blessed through children and that a man is happy when he has many sons.

> He gives the barren woman a home,
> making her the joyous mother of children. (Psalm 113:9)

> Sons are indeed a heritage from the Lord,
> the fruit of the womb a reward.
> Like arrows in the hand of a warrior
> are the sons of one's youth.
> Happy is the man who has his quiver full of them. (Psalm 127:3-5)

We often forget that infants were present during the significant history-making events of God's people. The sensory experience of these events—the sound, the touch, and the smell—had an impact on the faith formation of infants. Babies, as well as children, youth, and adults were a part of the covenant community that went out of Egypt into the wilderness. The faith of infants would have been formed and shaped during a pivotal time in the life of the nation of Israel. Infants would have heard the cries of their parents in captivity, would have heard the prayers of their parents as they crossed the sea to dry land, and would have listened to the victory song of Miriam as she stood on the banks of the seashore where she danced and played her tambourine. Infants would have wandered in the wilderness with the children of Israel, having their faith formed through the experiences of a nomadic lifestyle.

Moses was especially concerned about the faith formation of children. As the children of Israel got ready to enter the Promised Land, Moses wants to make sure that each generation is taught the ways of the Lord. Moses believed that faith must be passed along from generation to generation, taught in the midst of daily living.

> Hear, O Israel; The LORD is our God, the LORD alone. You shall love
> the LORD your God with all your heart, and with all your soul, and
> with all your might. Keep these words that I am commanding you
> today in your heart. Recite them to your children and talk about
> them when you are at home and when you are away, when you lie
> down and when you rise. Bind them as a sign on your hand, fix
> them as an emblem on your forehead, and write them on the door-
> posts of your house and on your gates. (Deuteronomy 6:4-9)

Parents are not the only ones instructed to pass along the faith. Children belong to a covenant community and all persons should be concerned with their faith formation. Jewish children of biblical times had opportunities throughout their lives to participate in the feasts of their faith. These feasts would have included infants who would have sensed the excitement and joyous celebration of family and community, even if these babies were too young to understand the stories of the faith. Children were not excluded from the faith community but participated along with the adults in the spiritual life of God's covenant people. By their very inclusion as infants, they were learning to trust in a community that cared for them and a God that loved them.

We learn some key concepts from the biblical view of children in the Old Testament, especially in the life of the nation of Israel, as it applies to our efforts at faith formation in the nursery.

- When infants come to our church nurseries, we need to welcome each child individually as a gift from God. These children are blessings to the entire church.
- We should count it a privilege, as well as a responsibility, to help shape the faith formation of these infants.
- Like Moses, leaders in the church must be concerned with the faith formation of all ages, recognizing that faith formation begins at birth.
- Choose caregivers who are persons of faith and who truly love and care for children. Volunteers should be carefully selected, and all of

these persons should be trained in understanding the faith formation of infants and children. We cannot expect our nursery workers
to help develop the faith formation of our children if they themselves do not have a strong faith to pass along.

- All of God's people in the faith community share the responsibility
  to be concerned for the faith formation of children. Efforts should
  be made to include persons of many generations to care for children
  in the nursery.
- Persons in your congregation who may not be the best qualified to
  work directly with the care of infants may nonetheless have the necessary gifts to make the nursery a better environment. Faith formation for infants should take place in the best possible atmosphere,
  and this means that the church nursery must be of the highest quality. Many persons who would not want to volunteer to care for
  infants can help make the nursery a welcoming, inviting space by
  using carpentry and sewing skills or offering financial support to
  purchase needed items.

An African proverbs states, "It takes a village to raise a child." The
nation of Israel believed that it was the responsibility of the entire community to raise a child in the Jewish faith. In the life of the church, we understand that it takes a congregation to raise a child. Guiding and nurturing a
child in faith formation in the church begins in the nursery, and it takes the
support and understanding of the entire congregation.

The way we treat these little ones, who cannot yet contribute to the life
of the congregation except with their smiles, laughter, cries, and hugs says
much about how we value children in the life of the church. If we start
these little ones out with our love and support, they will learn to trust
church as a happy place. This will carry over into their understanding of
God as One who can be trusted. The infant who is given the gift of strong
faith development will carry this foundation into childhood, youth, and the
adult years. Even if we are not directly involved in the nursery, we all need
to be concerned that infants and their parents are supported and valued.

New Testament Passages

The nation of Israel helped form the faith of infants because they allowed
children to be present with their parents and families during the pivotal
events that formed the faith identity of the people. Infants participated with
their siblings, parents, grandparents, relatives, and friends in the spiritual

life of the faith community. We see this pattern continuing in the stories we find in the New Testament. Children were present for the events in the life of Jesus and children were included in the home churches of the New Testament period.

Infants were present with their parents when Jesus told his parables on the hillside or the seashore. They felt the movement and excitement of their mother or father who carried them along with the crowds as they followed Jesus. They were present at the feeding of the five thousand. They heard the cries of "hosanna" on that first Palm Sunday. These infants did not understand the stories that Jesus was telling, but they understood from the tone of his voice that he was a kind and compassionate man. They did not comprehend the events in Jesus' life as they attended them with their parents, but they sensed deep within themselves that these were important times. Surely the senses came alive for these infants! Through the sounds, the smells, the touch, faith was being learned. Faith was being formed in a trusting environment. After all, their parents were there, listening and learning. The infants had learned to trust their parents and their parents had learned to trust this man Jesus, who took the time to bless their children.

Can you imagine what it was like to have been one of the children that were blessed by Jesus? This incident is recorded in Matthew, Mark, and Luke's gospels. (Matthew 19:13-15, Mark 10:13-16, Luke 18:15-17). In all three gospels, parents bring their children to Jesus so that He might touch them for a blessing. The disciples are indignant and try to keep the children away, but Jesus welcomes these children. Some of these children were no doubt babies as the Scriptures call them "little children." While there are similarities in the gospel accounts of Jesus blessing the children, Matthew is unique in telling us that the children had come to Jesus not only for a blessing but also for a prayer as well! Would we not want to know what words Jesus used as he prayed for these children? Surely his words of blessings would have let them know that they were loved. Did these parents share with their children, in years to come, what Jesus' prayer was for them that day? Did the children remember his gentle hands upon their head or his loving touch as he placed them in his arms? Faith formation was taking place for these children and infants as they learned how valued they were in the eyes of Jesus. Surely these children were among the first generation of Christians as they came of age in the faith.

Too often we are like those disciples, turning the children away and failing to realize their God-given potential for spiritual development. Before you take offense to this statement, be reminded that what we do in our church nurseries is an indication of how much we value children. We may not use harsh and indignant words, but we may fail to provide an atmosphere for infants that will help them grow in their faith.

Jesus not only blessed children, but he taught his disciples that they could not find true greatness in God's kingdom unless they were to humble themselves and become like little children. Jesus believed that children knew something that adults do not know. Children provide for us an example of how to enter the kingdom of God. Jesus said, "Truly I tell you, whoever does not receive the kingdom of God as a little child will never enter it." (Luke 18:17; Mark 10:15) A child comes to God in trust with childlike faith and this provides a model for those who wish to enter God's kingdom.

One of the most powerful passages of scripture about Jesus' teaching on children is found in Matthew 18:6-7. Jesus says, "If any of you put a stumbling block before one of these little ones who believe in me, it would be better for you if a great millstone were fastened around your neck and you were drowned in the depth of the seas." Here is an example in which Jesus uses children to speak of all persons who are without power in the society of his time. These little ones could include adults as well as children, but the point is that Jesus took the faith of children seriously. Jesus values children and their faith and holds them up as models of faith; they are to be imitated in our adult faith formation.[3]

These New Testament passages tell us about faith formation for infants and the vital role of the nursery in shaping the faith of children:

- When we do all we can in the church to make the nursery a welcoming, hospitable environment, we bless children as Jesus did. We offer them the opportunities to experience God's love in a caring place called the church nursery.
- Like the children who were present at the events in the life of Jesus, we provide infants the opportunity to use their senses through play and music and through touch, smell, and sound.
- We bless children in the church nursery when we care for their physical needs, knowing that meeting physical needs in a prompt, caring manner is the beginning of the developing ability of infants to trust others and God.
- The church nursery is a place where we can learn lessons from our children. Infants teach us how to trust. The infant is dependent on us to meet his or her needs just as we are dependent on God to meet our needs.

- Jesus gave worth and dignity to children. The church nursery is a place where we welcome and serve the little ones in our congregation whom we come to love and value as special children of God.

Nursery children are not spiritual beings apart from their social, physical, and emotional development. All of these aspects of children's personalities work together to make them the individuals they are and the individuals they are becoming. Luke 2:52 says, "And Jesus increased in wisdom and in years, and in divine and human favor." Jesus, who was born as a baby, experienced what all of our nursery children experience. He went through the developmental stages just like our children. How amazing to think that God came into human flesh as a baby and that our Savior went through the process of faith formation! Jesus experienced physical, spiritual, and emotional growth just as the children in our church are experiencing them as they grow from infancy to childhood, then as youth and adults!

This verse of Scripture in Luke 2:52 is the only summary we have of Jesus' developmental growth. We are given a concise picture of the relationship between body, mind, and spirit. Jesus, emerging from boyhood to youth, and then into adulthood, exemplifies a model of physical growth, moral insights, and character traits that are pleasing to those around him and to God. Jewish and Christian teachings are that the body, mind and spirit must be in a healthy relationship for one to become a whole person, of which Jesus is the prototype. This is why providing a nursery setting that takes into account the spiritual, physical, social, and emotional needs of the children is such a priority.

Our task can be a challenging one considering that most church nurseries do not serve just infants, but also toddlers, and, in some cases, preschool children. By the time children reach the age of five or six years, most churches have a kindergarten class. Many churches will also have a class for three- and four-year-olds, but not all. Some will still include them in the nursery area, perhaps with a separate nursery room for these preschool children. The ideal situation in the nursery is to have a room for infants, a room for toddlers, and, if needed, a room for the three and four years. In doing this, nursery workers are able to work with children who are in different stages of their spiritual, social, physical, and emotional development.

We have already mentioned several of the characteristics of infants and ways in which they develop spiritually. We need to consider the characteristics and spiritual development of older nursery children as well.

Characteristics and Spiritual Development of Older Nursery Children

Toddlers and Two-Year-Olds

As children enter the toddler and two years, they are able to communicate through the use of words. They are concrete, literal thinkers. Toddlers like repetition and they like a consistent schedule. They thrive on a routine. Nursery workers must be sure that the toddlers have the same schedule each time they come to the nursery. They like the same stories told to them time and again. They like the same songs about God, Jesus, and church played over and over again. This is the way that the toddler learns. When the toddler experiences the routine and safety of the nursery, he or she learns that it is a reliable place. The child associates this safe routine in the nursery with a God who is trustworthy and dependable.

The toddler needs to see the trustworthy face of a nursery worker who is there each week. Other persons may serve as volunteers, but it is important to have at least one worker that the toddler recognizes. As the child enters the toddler room of the nursery each week, he or she should do so knowing that he or she will find a familiar face in the nursery caregiver who loves the child and knows the child by name. Through this interaction, the child learns that God is always present and God knows the child by name.

Faith for the toddler or two-year-old is developed in the trusting, reliable routine of the nursery as workers play, pray, sing, tell and read stories, and interact with the child. These children are very egocentric. They think only about themselves, not about the other children in the nursery room. Workers can help the children begin to learn to share as they model for the children appropriate behavior. Sometimes this may mean protecting the child when another child is playing rough, biting, pulling hair, or taking away a toy the other child was playing with at the time. In other instances it may mean caring for a child who falls down or is injured.

Good nursery caregivers are also role models for the children. They show love for all children and should never show partiality to any child. They divide their time equally among the children. They remind children that they are to share with one another. They teach the valuable lesson that as children of God we are to express care and love to one another.

The two-year-old begins to associate God with the wonders around him or her. The nursery worker can point out pictures of God's creation or tell stories about God's wonderful world. The two-year-old can learn from the nursery caregiver that God takes care of me, that Jesus is my friend, and that the Bible is a special book. This is learned through music, stories, words, and pictures. A Bible can be present in the room that is kept in a special place and handled with great care and respect by the nursery workers.

Three- and Four-Year-Olds

As the child grows, he or she will be full of questions about God. Children learn spiritually by asking questions. Those working in the nursery should understand that when children ask questions, this is a teachable moment. Nursery workers need to respect the questions that children ask and take their questions seriously. Children reshape and redefine their understanding of God by the answers that they are given by their parents, teachers, and pastors.

Image of God

Psychoanalyst and author Ana-Marie Rizzuto conducted one of the most interesting studies on the way children grow spiritually. Rizzuto, in her clinical work, sought to refute the belief of psychologist Sigmund Freud that belief in God is based on a child's idea of his father. Rizzuto thought that the representation of God might come from a variety of sources and play a major part in the way one views the self, others, and the world. Rizzuto taught that children first become aware of God between the ages of two and three. She believed that these images of God are very powerful and remain with us throughout our lives. Rizzuto helped us to understand that a child's image of God was formed from many concrete elements in the child's life plus the child's own creative imagination. Imagination, play, experiences, and the influence of others all work together to help a child construct his or her image of God.[4]

Young children come to our congregations with their own image of God, outside of formal religious instruction. However, we have a vital, important role as their teachers and caregivers. We can help children rework their understanding of God. If the children have a destructive image in their understanding of God, hopefully teachers, parents, and nursery workers can introduce the children to new ideas about God. As we teach children in the home and church, we guide them to reshape their image of God. They learn about God from us and from their own experiences.

Coming to know God is a lifelong process. Caring adults can help children discover healthy images of God and erase destructive concepts that are not healthy for a vibrant faith. What nursery workers can do is to listen carefully as the older nursery children begin to talk about God. Listen especially for distorted, fearful images of God that focus on God's punishment. Nursery caregivers must assure children of God's love through stories, music, Bible pictures, and their own care and love for the children. As children are able to draw, they can express concepts of God that they are not always able to verbalize. Ask the children to share about the pictures they draw and talk with them about their concepts of God.

Questions of Nursery Children

Always answers questions as honestly as you can. Even the ones that seem unimportant to us are important to a child or they would not be asking them. Children can certainly ask challenging questions that sometimes leave us perplexed as how to answer. One way to help a child is to ask them, "What do you think?" In this way, you can more clearly understand where a child is coming from and perhaps answer the question that the child is really asking. Nursery and children's workers often make the mistake of giving children more of an answer than they needed or wanted. Keep the answers simple.

If you don't know the answer to a child's question, tell them you don't know. You may direct their questions to someone else who might provide an answer or simply let them know that there are some questions to which we have no answers. This helps children to understand that there is a mystery to our faith and some questions cannot be answered as easily as others.

Each Child Is Unique

In ministering to children in the nursery, we must journey along with children on their paths of faith. We must remember that each child is a unique individual and each child comes to faith in different ways, out of different life experiences. Children are born with the potential for spiritual quests, but each child will make his or her own discoveries based on the individual gifts and experiences of each child.

We cannot control how the Holy Spirit will work in the lives of our children. We can provide a safe, caring nursery environment. We can meet the needs of children, play with them, tell them Bible stories, sing to them, answer their questions, and engage their imaginations in spiritual matters. We can help them form a healthy image of God. Yet their relationship with

God will be their own. God is the one who takes the initiative to reach out and claim our children, as God's own. God is the One who extends grace and love. God is ultimately in charge of our children's spiritual formation. We must realize that the journey of faith is not separate from the journey of life. Children respond to God with their whole, emerging selves.

The challenge for our congregations is to recognize the importance of childhood as it relates to children as spiritual beings. We claim to value children, but do we? Most churches have understood adult spiritual formation apart from childhood spiritual formation. We have failed to understand the importance of spiritual formation for infants. Adult faith formation is the result of the faith formation we experienced as infants, children, and youth. That is one of the reasons the nursery is so very important. The lessons learned at the beginning of life: at home, in the community, and in the church nursery about God and faith are the stepping-stones to who we become as children of God throughout our spiritual journeys.

There are many lessons of faith to be learned in the church nursery! Could the church begin to help all of us in our faith journeys by applying these lessons about faith formation that we have learned from the nursery? Can the nursery be a model for the entire church of the ways in which the experiences of faith formation can strengthen all of us? What we do in the nursery can have an impact on the entire church in the area of faith formation!

The Church Can Learn From the Nursery in the Area of Faith Formation

Trust

- As the child leaves the nursery, he or she will begin the process of going from one age-level class to the other. Teachers and leaders of children and youth must build on the foundation of trust that children have experienced in the nursery.
- All persons need opportunities for small group learning where leaders are competent, trustworthy individuals. They may find these leaders in Sunday school classes, Bible study group, men and women's groups, small groups, and support groups within the church.
- Infants are not the only ones who transfer trust or lack of trust from other persons to God. Some children, youth, and adults have been through life experiences where they have been abused physically, mentally, or emotionally. Other persons may have the experience of

divorce and betrayal or may have lived in situations of addiction. Many have faced difficult circumstances where their trust in others has been shattered. Pastors and church leaders must find ways through support groups, sermons, and Bible lessons to help persons who lack trust in other persons, and even lack trust in God.

Faith Experiences for All Ages

- These include Bible studies, Sunday school classes, fellowship events, and support groups.
- All persons should be given opportunities for sensory learning, including visual experiences (maps, charts, time-lines, models, illustrations) and auditory experiences (CDs, music, movie clips). Teachers can bring in examples of items from the lesson for persons to touch or have students cook and taste Bible foods.
- Faith development for our entire congregation must be carried out in an organized, planned, deliberate, and intentional manner.
- We are spiritual beings, but not apart from physical, social, emotional, and moral development. Faith formation for all persons in the church should take into account not just the spiritual aspect, but the physical, social, emotional, and moral needs.
- Faith development experiences are best carried out in relationship with others.
- Knowing a person's name and affirming him or her as a person of worth and self-esteem is important.
- Small groups, Sunday school classes, and support groups are often the places where people can engage in relationships with others and be recognized as persons of value. We need classes that are age-based and some classes that are needs-based (such as caring for aging parents, divorce support, addiction, marriage support, sexuality issues for children/youth, etc.).
- It is essential for teachers to be trained in faith development for each age level. Training should be given on the spiritual, physical, social, and emotional needs of each age level in the church. Life issues and concerns that each age-level group is facing or will be facing in the future needs to be studied and groups provided to offer support at each phases of the life cycle.
- Like the nursery child, we are all self-centered and sometimes see ourselves as the center of the universe. Some psychologists believe that we move out of this egocentric stage as we grow older. We need

ways to express our faith that allow us to move beyond our egocentric nature. In planning faith development experiences, churches must allow individual ways to work and relate to others and to be a part of mission endeavors that share with others.

- Our faith development does not come about in isolation. We need others in the community of faith to love us, support us, and hold us accountable. Like the nursery children, we need teachers, mentors, and friends. It takes a congregation to raise a child and to raise all of us!

Meeting Physical Needs

- Physical needs in congregations can be met through sporting events and exercise programs. Just as important is the physical appearance of the classrooms and the sanctuary of the church. Rooms should be neat with age-appropriate furniture and furnishing.
- We can share with church leaders, particularly those in charge of the physical care of our church building, that all persons need a physical environment that is conducive to learning. We may point out, "Now that we have done this in the nursery area and we know the positive results for our infants, let's do the same for other age-levels in our church."
- Remind those in charge of the church facilities that when physical needs are met, we also aid in spiritual development. You can use the nursery as a starting point to advocate for other spaces in the church being cleaned out and made to look inviting and welcoming for church members.

Sensory Learning

- The church sanctuary should be a place where symbols are used as visual aids to help person learn through the use of their senses. Symbols of our faith such as the cross, banners, and stained glass windows all help in faith development.
- Encourage Sunday school teachers to allow students of all ages to use their senses in learning.
- Churches must find ways for adults, youth, and children to understand the symbols of the church and to participate in the rituals of the church.

Struggles in Our Faith

- We lay the foundation in the nursery, but we must help teachers of preschool, elementary, youth, and adult age levels to understand how important questions are as persons struggle with faith issues.
- Taking seriously the questions that the older nursery children (twos and beyond) ask us is important. So are the questions of all persons in our church.
- Challenging questions should not be ignored, but dealt with in a compassionate, biblical, and truthful manner to the best of our abilities.

Image of God

- Children, youth, and adults come to our churches with an image of God that may be distorted. This image has been constructed through our experiences and the teachings of the church. Teachers, leaders, and pastors must help members correct and reshape images of God that are unhealthy and unbiblical.
- Conversations with others in the faith often are the ways in which persons begin to form positive images of God. Teachers and leaders must listen carefully to what people are saying about God. This is especially true for the teachers of children.
- Youth may also bring to the church images of God that are not biblical. Youth are affected by media images and past childhood experiences that may have distorted their image of a loving, caring God. Those who work with youth must be sensitive to the needs, hurts, and concerns of this age group and do all they can to affirm young people as they struggle with their image of God.
- Adults may form an image of God out of past experiences and present situations, and often have a hard time shaking the image of God learned in childhood. This adult needs mature teachers, mentors, and friends who will help them grow in their faith development and reshape their image of God if needed.

Our biblical understanding of the value of children can be applied to the ways we treat all of God's children, both inside and outside the church. Just as Jesus blessed little children and gave them a place of priority in God's kingdom, Jesus also blesses his children of all ages.

Throughout the Old and New Testament, children were included in the covenant community. This understanding of the importance of children to the faith communities in the Bible must be extended to all persons. Faith formation is molded, in large part, by a community of faith where we are valued for who we are as children of God. We should all be given a place of priority in the church community.

The love and care that we show our nursery children is an extension of the love and care that God shows for each of us. The way we treat these little ones provides a powerful image to the entire church of the way we are treated by God and the way in which we should treat one another as brothers and sisters in Christ.

Infants teach us how to trust God and one another. We come to trust when we are a part of a congregation that cares about our faith development at each stage of our life. We come to trust when this congregation meets our needs. We come to trust when we learn about a God who is faithful at all times and all places in our life journey.

One of the reasons the church nursery is the most important space in the church is that what is being provided for infants in the area of faith formation is so vitally important for the entire church. The lessons taught and modeled are powerful lessons for your congregation. Learn from them and use them!

Chapter Two Endnotes

1. Erik Erickson, *Childhood and Society* (New York: W. W. Norton, 1963), 249-250.
2. Scottie May, Beth Posterski, Catherine Stonehouse, & Linda Cannell, *Children Matter: Celebrating Their Place In the Church, Family, and Community* (Grand Rapids, Michigan: William B. Eerdan Publishing Co., 2005), 27-28.
3. Ibid., 42-43.
4. Ana-Maria Rizzuto, *The Birth of the Living God: A Psychoanalytic Study* (Chicago: University of Chicago Press, 1979), 122, 187.

Chapter Three

WELCOME MAT

Extending Hospitality in the Nursery & Congregation

Meet Jason and Sally Martin. Jason and Sally, a young couple in their early 30s, were married eight years ago. They have tried, unsuccessfully, for several years to have a child. They are active members of a local congregation and attend a young adult Sunday school class. In their Sunday school class, they have shared openly about their desire to have children. They have also shared honestly about some of the problems they have faced as Sally has tried time and again to get pregnant. The class has prayed with them and encouraged them. Finally, they decided to try fertility treatments, hoping that Sally might get pregnant. They are delighted when, after some time, they discover Sally is pregnant. Then, they are shocked when the doctor tells them that they are going to be the parents of triplets!

The Sunday school class continues to pray and offer support to Jason and Sally during Sally's pregnancy, which turns out to be difficult. Near the end of her pregnancy, Sally is ordered to get bed-rest by her doctor, so her activities are very restricted. Sally and Jason's Sunday school class delivers meals to the home weekly, continuing this ministry of care and concern throughout Sally's pregnancy. One of the women's circles in the church holds a baby shower for the couple. Several ladies and some men in the church take an interest in the upcoming birth and agree to help the couple after the babies are born. They work out a rotating schedule and these adopted grandparents prepare to take turns helping the couple as soon as the babies arrive.

When the babies are born, pastors and friends visit the couple in the hospital. A rose is placed on the altar in honor of the babies' birth and their arrival is joyfully shared during the morning worship service. The newsletter carries an announcement about the birth of the babies. The adopted grandparents get busy helping the family, and continue to do this for a year after the babies are born.

The babies are welcomed into the church nursery where they are called by name and cared for lovingly in a warm, pleasant environment. After a few months, the triplets are baptized, and the church family vows to help the parents raise the children in the Christian faith, a vow many of the church members have put into practice even before the children were born.

This is hospitality at its best. Even though the names of the parents have been changed, this is a true story of how one church welcomed triplets into the life of its congregation. At whatever point infants enter the life of your congregation, your congregation should graciously welcome these children, their parents, and other family members.

Our understanding of hospitality stems from what we know about the very nature of God. God is a God of hospitality. Time and again God reaches out to each of us in love, calling us by name, and welcoming us to be in relationship with our God. The Scriptures tell us that God knows us by name. The prophet Isaiah speaks of a God who made us. We belong to God.

> But now thus says the LORD,
> he who created you, O Jacob,
> he who formed you, O Israel:
> Do not fear, for I have redeemed you;
> I have called you by name, you are mine. (Isaiah 43:1)

Not only does God know us by name, but the Scriptures also indicate to us that God knew us before we were even born. When God called Jeremiah to become a prophet to his people, God assured Jeremiah that he knew him in his mother's womb.

> "Before I formed you in the womb I knew you,
> and before you were born I consecrated you;
> I appointed you a prophet to the nations." (Jeremiah 1:5)

Jeremiah had a special calling as a prophet of God, yet this does not lessen the call God has for each of us. Just as God knew Jeremiah before he was born, God knows all of us. This is especially important as we consider welcoming infants into the life of the church and the church nursery. We must remember that God's grace and love extended to these infants before their birth. We extend hospitality to them in response to God's radical hospitality offered even before they are born. We also extend hospitality to infants as we recognize God's continuing grace at work in their lives.

The Scriptures present a picture of Jesus welcoming children, many of whom were infants. Not only does Jesus welcome the children, but he also teaches his disciples that the act of welcoming children is an act of greatness. In Matthew 18:1-5, the disciples come to Jesus and ask him who is the greatest in God's kingdom. Jesus calls a child and places this child in the midst of the disciples. He instructs his disciples that they must change and become like children. He then says, "Whoever welcomes one such child in my name welcomes me." (Matthew 18:5)

When we welcome children into the church nursery, when we call them by name, and when do all we can to make the nursery a welcoming place, we are also welcoming Jesus. To welcome and care for their parents and family members is to welcome the presence of the Christ who blessed children.

Our church nursery is the entry point for children to begin their faith journey in the church, but also the place where they enter the life of the faith community. From their nursery experience, infants will be introduced into the life of the congregation. Will they learn that your church is a warm, inviting place? They will pick up on this message if you go out of your way to welcome the baby, love the baby, care for the baby, and meet the baby's needs in the church nursery. However, if you do not welcome the baby into the nursery, do not know his or her name, and do not meet the child's basic needs in a prompt manner, then the baby will quickly understand that the church nursery is not a welcoming place. It will not take a baby long to know that he or she would rather be any place except the church nursery.

Parents can sense when the child's nursery experience has been a pleasant one. They can also sense when the child is upset and does not like the nursery. If the child does not have a good experience in the nursery, the parents are very likely not going to return to your church. Yet, if the baby is happy in the nursery, parents will probably continue to worship in your congregation if both the child and the family's needs are met.

Churches should welcome the child into the life of the congregation from the moment he or she is born. When the child is born, the pastors should make an effort to visit in the hospital or home, offering a blessing upon the child and family. Pastors can take a gift to the family. A small New Testament Bible is an appropriate gift. Recognition of the birth of the child should be placed in the newsletter. Some churches choose to place a rose on the altar in honor of the birth of the child.

If the child's parents are involved in a Sunday school class, the choir, the women's or men's group, or another group within the church, efforts should be made to see that this group provides meals for the family for at least a month. If the parents do not have a Sunday school class, contact the young adult class that the parents might want to be a part of once they are able to again become active in the life of the church. Providing meals for the family is not only a great help, but lets parents know their class or group truly welcomes their child. If the parents do not belong to a class or group, but a class or group goes out of its way to provide meals, this gives the parents a sense of welcome and provides them some needed contacts in the church. Very likely this couple will attend the class that has extended such welcome and hospitality to their family.

Pastors, staff, and other church members should take time to contact the family occasionally to see how they are doing and if they have any needs. Let the family know that you look forward to having the family and baby attend church as soon as they are able. Give them information about the nursery program and information about infant baptism or child dedication. Pass information about the family and newborn along to the child-care worker in your church nursery so that person can be prepared to welcome the baby and family when they arrive at the nursery for the first time.

Pastors and others should record the date of the birth of the baby. Send a note on the child's first birthday. You can recognize all of the infants born in your congregation during the Advent season by presenting the families with a "Baby's First Christmas" ornament. Families and babies can come to the altar for the presentation and for a prayer of blessing.

Many parents of newborns are hesitant to leave their child in the church nursery, particularly if this is their first child. When you learn that a family is expecting a child, invite them to visit the nursery and get to know the nursery workers. This will help to alleviate some of the anxiety they feel. Do not pressure these parents to leave their child in the nursery if they do not feel comfortable doing so. Yet, if you have made your nursery a welcoming place, parents will be much more likely to leave their child. Do let them know about the nursery and that the infant is welcome at any time.

All infants should be welcomed to the church nursery by the pleasant, calming voice of a childcare worker. The child should be called by name. Remind nursery caregivers that God knows all of our names and the name of the child. Therefore, we must make every effort to know the names of the nursery children and their parents' names.

Welcome Packet

Provide a welcome packet for parents the first time they arrive at the nursery with their child. In the packet include a card that parents can fill out and return to the nursery, giving information about the family and the child. The packet should include information about the nursery policy. If you have a parent's day out program or day care, include information about these programs. You might add a gift from the church.

Sign-In Sheet & Information Card

One of the ways you welcome children in the nursery is to provide a sign-in sheet and information card. The sign-in sheet should be used each time the nursery is open. Parents put down the names of the child, along with any needs or concerns. They also let the childcare workers know where the parents can be found while they are in the church building. For example, ask what class the parents will be attending during the Sunday school time so that you could find them in the event of an emergency. Parents should also indicate who has permission to pick up the child from the nursery.

Parents should fill out the information card the first time they arrive at the church nursery. This card should contain information about the child and parents such as address, phone number, allergies, food needs, special care needs, and other relevant information. Keep these cards on file in the nursery. Even though these are housekeeping details, they communicate to the parents that you are concerned about the welfare of the children in the nursery. Good records and information serve as a means of welcome.

Smaller churches or congregations who know each other well may feel it is not necessary to have a sign-in sheet for the nursery. However, it is comforting for parents when nursery workers know the name of their child and that the child is well identified. Parents can relax, worship, study, and fellowship at your church when they know that the nursery workers know the parents' names and where to find them in an emergency situation.

Mark Belongings

Another way you welcome children is by encouraging parents to mark all of the child's belongings so that you can keep up with them. Each child should have his or her own shelf in the church nursery where diaper bags can be placed. Place the name of the nursery child on his or her shelf and have extra spaces for visitors.

Parents become very frustrated when the child's possessions are not cared for or get lost. Identifying all diaper bags, sippy cups, bottles, and personal belongings lets the parents know that you care.

Safety Issues

Safety is always a concern for parents. Nursery workers should know who has permission to pick up children in the church nursery. Churches should have updated policies on fire and weather-related emergencies. All members of the church need to know about these policies and what to do in the event of an emergency. Have a practice emergency drill so all Sunday school classes know where to go what to do in the event of fire or a weather-related emergency.

Why are the actions of implementing these emergency policies so important as far as the nursery is concerned? In the event of an emergency, parents of nursery children would be instructed not to rush to the nursery to pick up their child. Trained nursery workers would have the responsibility of getting nursery children out of the building in the event of a fire or to a designated safe place in the event of a weather-related emergency. Parents who rush to the nursery in an emergency situation create more havoc and chaos. Having a policy in place and training parents and nursery workers in this policy, as well as having a fire/emergency drill will help alleviate the concern parents have about safety measures.

Be sure there is a first-aid kit in the room and that nursery workers are trained in CPR and first aid procedures.

There should always be a phone in the church nursery with emergency numbers posted nearby. Nursery workers should be discouraged from using their cell phones for personal calls while they are working the nursery. This can often be a problem when youth are working as volunteers. Make it clear to all workers that cell phones are not allowed in the nursery. The paid nursery worker in charge may have one available in the case of emergency, but other workers should not bring their cell phones into the nursery or shut them off so they will not ring and bother the children.

Have your Trustees check on the doors near the nursery area. Some churches choose to lock these doors during the worship service for safety reasons; to make sure strangers cannot enter. Ushers should be trained in checking the nursery area during worship for safety concerns.

Some congregations provide beepers for parents or have other safety measures. Whatever you do, make sure that parents feel comfortable leaving their children in the church nursery.

Policies for Illness

Just as important as the safety policies are the policies you set for illness in the nursery. Develop guidelines for sick children so that parents know when they may bring the child to the nursery and when to keep them at home. Inform other parents in the nursery if you learn that a child present in the nursery has a contagious illness. It is difficult to tell parents they cannot bring a child to the nursery, but you want to create the most welcoming, healthy environment for the children.

Nursery policies should be available in writing. This includes matters such as safety, discipline, child-worker ratios, and other pertinent information about the church nursery. These policies should be given to the parents the first time they arrive at the nursery door.

Conditions of the Nursery

Experts in church growth inform us that one of the primary reasons that young families choose or reject a church is due to the condition of the church nursery. A clean nursery is a welcoming sign. Even classroom doors should be inviting since this is the first part of the nursery parents will approach. Putting pictures of the children and teachers on the church door is a welcoming sign. Be sure and take a picture of the first time a new child comes to the nursery. Take pictures throughout the year and keep a scrapbook for the nursery that the parents will enjoy seeing. When a child is baptized, obtain a picture of the child, together with his or her parents, and the pastor. Display this photograph in the church nursery.

The church nursery should be spotless. Clean sheets should be on the cribs. Furniture and toys should be checked for safety and should be age appropriate. Rockers, swings, and playpens should be up to date. There should be good lighting in the room. Outlets should be covered. Cabinet latches should be placed on lower cabinets. Diaper pails should be emptied out as needed so the nursery smells nice.

Murals can be painted on the walls that are attractive and colorful. Carpets should be vacuumed and cleaned on a regular basis. There should be attractive curtains on the windows and if there are blinds in the room, make sure the chords are shortened so older nursery children cannot pull on them. Be sure the walls are painted with paint that is not lead-based. Murals and paint colors should be selected that are soothing and not too bright or stimulating.

The trustees of the church should know about the operations of the nursery. Challenge your trustees to take a tour of the nursery from the standpoint of the child. Have the trustees get down on their knees and look at the nursery from the view of the child. Look for any dangers to the infants and toddlers. Especially have them look for sharp edges around the room that could injure a child. Trustees should also check the room temperature to be sure it is comfortable. Trustees need to take a look at the church insurance policy. They should make sure that any injuries that may occur in the church nursery are covered by the policy.

The trustees should also be sure that bathroom facilities are adequate for the nursery area. A sink should be low enough for toddlers and twos so they can wash their own hands. A potty-chair should be available.[1]

Nursery workers should look clean and neat. Some churches require that nursery workers wear aprons. Instruct nursery workers not to wear earrings that children might pull or jewelry that might scratch children. Nursery workers should wear comfortable clothes and shoes, but they should look well groomed.

Nursery workers or the nursery committee should clean the toys regularly and check for any loose parts that might choke a child. Get rid of any dangerous toys.

All of these housekeeping matters say to the child and parent, "Welcome." You may have never thought of the condition of the nursery itself as a means of welcome and hospitality, but besides the greeting of the nursery workers, the environment will be the first impression a parent has of your nursery. The condition of the nursery says either "we welcome your child" or "we do not really care about your child."

Having done all of these things, you may feel that your nursery is now a welcoming place. Yes, doing all of these tasks will assure that your nursery is a welcoming place. Yet we must also consider some special considerations that will ensure all children feel welcomed.

Children & Parents with Special Concerns

You may have children in your nursery from a variety of ethnic groups. Especially by the age of two, your nursery children will begin to recognize physical differences such as skin color and body size. Remember that children will be influenced by the attitudes of those who care for them. Children can pick up on spoken and unspoken messages. Caregivers in the nursery must learn to respect cultural differences. Toilet training, feeding, the way a child plays, and expressions are influenced by one's cultural background. Caregivers must be sensitive to the cultural background of children. They should always welcome children of any race or background to the church nursery.[2]

The same welcome you give to all children who come to the church nursery should be given to children with special needs. Talk with the parents of special needs children to learn the most effective way to care for them in the nursery. It may be that you will need to have one nursery volunteer whose has the sole responsibility of caring for a special needs child. There may be a person in the congregation who is trained to care for special needs children. This person might be a volunteer in the nursery or help you understand how to care for the special needs child.

We must also consider the parents of nursery children. Some of these may be single parents. You may have a single mother who has never married, but has chosen to raise her child alone, perhaps with the help of other family members. There may be a single parent who has divorced, but has custody of the child. In other situations, there may be a single divorced parent who has visitation rights on certain weekends and brings the baby to the church nursery only on visitation weekends. Go out of your way to make these parents feel welcome. Find ways to help these persons integrate into the life of the church through young adult Sunday school classes or support groups for divorced or single parents.

Other Ideas

We welcome parents and young children into our congregation when we provide childcare for all worship services, meetings, and programs. We welcome them when we provide highchairs and booster seats at our congregational meals. We welcome them when we provide a separate room near the sanctuary where parents can take young children during the worship service who may be crying or upset. We welcome parents and young children when we provide a private place for a new mother to nurse her child and change diapers. Some churches even provide rockers in the back of the sanctuary for parents to rock children during the service or booster seats for young children who cannot see when they sit on the church pews. You can come up with creative ideas on ways to welcome parents and young children.

Suggestions for Providing Welcome in the Church Nursery

1. Have nursery workers contact expectant parents and invite them to tour the nursery.
2. Place a rose on the altar to welcome new babies born in your congregation and put information about the birth of a child in the newsletter and bulletin.
3. Provide meals for new parents for at least a month.
4. Provide parents a welcome packet that contains nursery information, nursery guidelines, nursery policies, and information about safety.
5. Have a sign-in sheet for the nursery so nursery workers know where parents are while they are in the church facility.
6. Have parents fill out information cards giving their name, address, phone number, email, and other pertinent information. Include a place for parents to indicate if the child has allergies, medical conditions, or special diets.
7. Have safety measures in place: first aid kits, and phone in each nursery room. Check furniture and equipment in the nursery for safety. Put safety covers on all outlets. If you have beepers, be sure parents know how to use them and that there are enough for visitors.
8. Have Trustees do a thorough check of the nursery for safety concerns. Have them get down on the eye level of the nursery children.
9. Have parents mark all of the child's belongings and keep them in a cubby marked with the child's name. Have extra cubbies for visitors.
10. Have specific guidelines for illness in the nursery so parents are clear when they should not bring their child to the nursery.
11. Have nursery workers respect the cultural background of each child.
12. Take into account the needs of single and divorced parents.
13. Start a Home Visitor program. Parents are visited in the home and

provided information about parenting and the home visitor learns of any needs or concerns of the parents.

14. Link new parents with experienced parents in your church.
15. Have a library of books and video materials that will help parents with parenting skills, discipline, and guiding their children in spiritual formation.
16. Be sure the nursery is inviting, clean, and cheerful.
17. Be sure nursery workers are pleasant and call children and parents by name. Be sure nursery workers are well groomed.
18. Provide childcare for all worship services, meetings, and programs at your church.
19. Provide highchairs and booster seats at fellowship dinners.
20. Have a "cry room" (a room where parents can take upset children, but can still hear or view the worship service).
21. Provide a private room for mothers to nurse.
22. Provide rocking chairs at the back of your sanctuary.
23. Provide booster seats for toddlers and young children to sit in during worship.
24. Present families of infants a Christmas ornament during Advent to celebrate their child's first Christmas. Have a prayer of blessing in worship with the infant and family as you present the ornament.
25. Place pictures of nursery children on a board. Take pictures of children when they are baptized or dedicated.
26. Begin an adopted grandparent program in your church. Be sure and include nursery children in this program.
27. Highlight your Parent's Day Out program or daycare program and provide information to parents of nursery children.
28. Be sure nursery workers welcome visiting parents of the children who come to your church. Have the workers pass along information about visitors to the church staff for follow-up.
29. Encourage your pastor or other minister/staff members to walk by the nursery occasionally and greet workers, parents, and children.

What Your Church Can Learn From the Church Nursery

Welcome

When visitors come into our church doors, we should welcome them. Have friendly greeters and ushers who have been trained. Use attractive signs that point the way to classes, the restrooms, and the nursery. Have persons available to take visitors to Sunday school classes and introduce them to the teachers and other members. Introduce visitors to church members who invite the visitors to sit with them in church. We can even do this before the visitor gets to the doors of the church by providing visitor parking spots and greeters in the church parking lot to help visitors. These are ways to say, "Welcome to our church, we are glad you are here."

The way we welcome children who visit our churches says a great deal to visitors about the way we value children in our congregation. Children should be greeted as well as adults. Families should be introduced to persons who have children. Worship bags, containing an age appropriate bulletin, crayons, and maybe a devotional book, can be provided for children during the worship services. Be sure children who visit are given one of these bags. Many times we forget that visiting children are not aware of our regular activities for the children of our church. Instruct visiting children on what to do if you have a children's sermon during worship or a Children's Worship time and invite them to any weekly children's activities.

Know Names

Just as it is important to know the names of the children in the nursery, we need to know the names of visitors and church members. Visitors to the church are very impressed when you can call them by name. Pastors should make every effort to review the names of visitors, but greeters and others in the church can do this as well. A phone call, a note, or a gift from the church during the week is an additional means of welcome.

Knowing the names of persons in our Sunday school classes and other groups is vitally important. Many years ago, the United Methodist Church had a Sunday school emphasis entitled, "Where Everybody Knows My Name," by which teachers were reminded of the importance of getting to know the names of the people in their classes. However, we must get to know the persons themselves as well. Learning about the occupation, interests, and concerns of persons in our Sunday school classes is a way of welcoming.

Radical Hospitality

We may find it easy to welcome visitors and church members when they look, talk, and act like the majority of our congregation. However, as we have welcomed all children into the church nursery, we must welcome all persons into the life of the church. Are we willing to welcome persons who are physically and mentally challenged? Are we willing to welcome persons who face addictions? Will we open the doors of our church to groups such as Alcoholics Anonymous, Narcotics Anonymous or groups dealing with sexual addiction, gambling addiction, or eating disorders? Would we be willing to welcome a homeless person into our congregation or a person of another race or culture? If we believe that all of us are God's children, then we must reexamine the way we carry out hospitality in our churches.

In the parable of the sheep and goats, Christ mentions that the way we treat the persons in our society who are without status or power determines we way we treat Christ himself. Mentioned in the parable are the poor, the hungry, the prisoner, and the stranger. (Matthew 25:31-46) In the parable, Jesus says, "Truly I tell you, just as you did it to one of the least of these who are members of my family, you did it to me." Nursery children are among the least of these, but so are persons who are poor, homeless, addicted, or even the stranger who comes to visit our churches. Will we welcome these persons like we welcome the little ones in our nursery?

Crisis Prevention

The support we offer nursery parents should extend to the parents of children and youth within our church. We can offer parenting classes, marriage and divorce seminars, and workshops on childhood and youth issues, and support groups. Just as we reach out and begin our ministry with expectant parents, even before the baby is born, we need to be alert in the church to sense when families of our children and youth are facing crisis in their lives. For example, we may learn that a family is having martial problems. The pastor can provide counseling or suggest marriage counselors in the community. We should not wait until the problems escalate and it is too late to help.

Condition of Church & Safety Issues

Walk around the halls and classrooms of the church. Remove clutter, paint walls, and see that the classrooms have furnishing and supplies that meet the age-level needs of the group. Churches can have a workday at the church to involve all members in cleaning and repair work.

Just as we have been concerned about safety issues in the nursery, we need to check out safety issues for all ages in the church. Locking furnace rooms, the janitor's supply closet, and other dangerous areas of the church for safety shows you care. So is making sure that cutting boards and office equipment are kept away from children. If you have an elevator in your church, you need to have policies on whether children can use them by themselves or whether adults need to be present for supervision.

Tour your church to see if it is accessible to the handicapped or older adults. Get a wheelchair and have someone sit in it. Push them up the handicap ramp or go around tight spots in your church to see if a wheelchair can get through. Be sure and have a wheelchair available at the church for use by those who may need it.

Do you have a step for children to use when drinking from water fountains or do you have a water fountain that is short enough for children? Do youth have a space in the church decorated by them, a space that is warm and inviting? Are the classrooms well lit? Are the restrooms clean? Do senior adults have a room with comfortable chairs? What we do in the nursery to provide for a child's basic needs should continue throughout the church.

Care for All Ages

Children must be made to feel welcome to participate in the life of the church. Children can usher, pass out bulletins, help clean up the church, read Scripture, acolyte, and engage in mission projects.

Let youth take an active part in the life of the church. They need leaders who provide role models of Christian maturity and they need opportunities to serve.

Singles need the support of the church. If you do not have many singles in your church, you can link them with other churches so activities can be planned with a larger group of singles.

Senior adults need to be affirmed and valued for their wisdom and contributions to the life of the church. Active senior adults enjoy a fellowship group outside of Sunday school where they can meet for meals, programs, and trips.

Don't forget about the homebound or sick in your congregation. They, too, need to be extended hospitality and love. A recording of the service can provide these homebound members with a way to participate in worship. Members can deliver the tapes along with a bulletin. On Communion Sunday, arrange to have communion, which has been blessed in your worship service, delivered to the homebound. You can provide liturgy and prayers that the visitation team can use when sharing communion with your homebound. Set up a regular visitation program in your church to have all ages reach out to the homebound.

Hospitality through Holy Communion

One of the most powerful ways your congregation can extend hospitality is through Holy Communion. In many traditions, the Lord's Table is open to all persons regardless of age, race, church membership, or religious background. All are welcome to come and experience God's grace and love. When we come to the table of our Lord we come as equals. We come as children of God. Like the children in our nursery we come needing to be fed, to be loved, and to be embraced by a Caregiver who reaches out to us with protective arms. At the table we meet a God of hospitality who welcomes us.

Even before we are born God has claimed us and knows us by name. This God of hospitality invites us and calls us to extend hospitality to others. Does your church have the gift of hospitality? If not, a good starting point is the church nursery. Begin there, but recognize that hospitality is contagious. What starts in the church nursery cannot be contained in one space in the church. Hospitality will quickly spread to other areas of your church life. Hospitality is a gift from God and God's gifts are to be shared in the church, in the community, and in the world.

Chapter Three Endnotes

1. Mary Alice Gran, "Room Size and Location," in *The First Three Years: A Guide for Ministry with Infants, Toddlers & Two-Year-Olds*, ed. Mary Alice Gran (Nashville: Discipleship Resources, 1989), 81.

2. Mary Pat Martin, "All God's Children Valuing Diversity," in *The First Three Years: A Guide for Ministry with Infants, Toddlers & Two-Year-Olds*, ed. Mary Alice Gran (Nashville: Discipleship Resources, 1989), 73.

MORE THAN NURSERY RHYMES
Nurture in the Nursery & Faith Community

A children's minister was very excited as she told her nursery committee that she had found new ways to help nurture and teach the nursery children. She had been looking through her denomination's catalogue when she discovered some curriculum and music that she believed would be excellent resources for the nursery. She noticed some Bible picture cards that she knew would be age appropriate for use in the toddler nursery. They contained a short Bible story, a song that the nursery workers could sing to the children, and ideas listed on the card that parents could use at home to reinforce the teaching in the nursery.

The children's minister was also interesting in ordering several CDs that contained lullabies and songs for use with infants and toddlers. She suggested to her nursery committee that she would be willing to lead a workshop to help the nursery workers understand how to teach the children through music, play, words, and stories and how to incorporate the curriculum for use in the Sunday morning nursery program. She reminded the committee that at the present time, the nursery workers were doing nothing more than babysitting. She believed that, with proper training, they could do much more to nurture the nursery children.

This children's minister met with opposition from her nursery committee. They believed what was happening in the church nursery adequately met the needs of the children. There was certainly no reason for a change. One committee member asked, "Are not nursery children too young to learn much of anything about God?" Another said, "Why in the world would we want to spend money on Bible picture cards? What we are doing now is just fine."

While the nursery committee in this church had worked very hard to develop nursery policies and had taken seriously the task of providing a nursery environment that was welcoming, they did not see the need for the request made by the children's minister. The daunting task ahead for the children's minister will be to help the committee understand that there is more to the nursery than babysitting. She must also teach them that although providing a quality environment and welcoming children are important, there is more to be done in the nursery.

The effective church nursery is a place where children learn and where they can be nurtured in the faith. Yet until this children's minister can change the minds of her nursery committee about the need for nurture in the nursery, her requests will be ignored.

How can nursery caregivers nurture faith? What can caregivers do to help children learn? Is there a need for curriculum of any kind in the nursery? These are some of the questions that will have to be answered before the children's minister will be able to convince her nursery committee of the need for Bible picture cards, music CDs, or for her training workshop.

The church nursery is the first place in your church that a child's faith will be nurtured. Nursery caregivers have a huge task when we consider that we are asking them to meet children's needs, model appropriate behavior, nurture children, and teach children.

One of the most important gifts you can provide nursery children and parents is a qualified, competent, loving nursery worker. Most often this person will be paid. Be careful in your selection of the nursery worker who will be in charge of the nursery. Look for a mature individual who demonstrates a sense of calm. Train this person in understanding developmental characteristics of nursery children. Help this person and all other volunteers in the nursery to understand that working in the nursery is more than babysitting. Children are learning, and they are dependent on others to help nurture their faith.

Children are natural learners. Children learn very quickly in the early years of life and in many ways, mostly by doing and experiencing. Infants and toddlers learn from watching, listening, playing, exploring, and trying new things.

When nursery children are nurtured and guided to grow in their faith in healthy ways, they develop a desire to know God and enter into a relationship with God. We nurture children in different ways depending on the child's age and developmental level.

The primary area for the nurture of children should be the Christian home. Churches certainly recognize that not all homes are centers for faith formation. Even in families where parents desire to be pivotal in faith formation for their children, these parents often feel inadequate. The church must partner with the home to nurture children in the faith. Churches can provide resources for parents to use in the home to share faith with children. These can include Bible readings, mealtime and bedtime prayers, and activities in which the family can participate together. When we nurture children, we nurture their parents. When we partner with the home to teach children the faith, we nurture families. Working together, the nursery setting, the church, and the family can nurture children and help them grow in faith.

Our understanding of nurture is rooted in the ways God nurtures each of us. A picture of God as nurturer is found in Hosea 11:1-11. The prophet Hosea shares with us one of the most beautiful and moving passages of God's covenant love toward an unfaithful people.

When Israel was a child, I loved him,
and out of Egypt I called my son.
The more I called them, the more they went from me;
they kept sacrificing to the Ba'als,
and offering incense to idols. (Hosea 11:1-2)

This passage reminds us of the ways in which God's people, in all times and places, have been unfaithful to our Nurturer. God calls us as God's children and our obligation as sons and daughters is to be faithful. Yet we rebel and fail to hold up our part of the covenant. We act as ungrateful children. So with the realization that God, our loving Parent, has done all God can do to nurture, God accepts the responsibility of a Parent who must also discipline. God knows that discipline is necessary, but God's love for us is over-powering. So God offers forgiveness and the opportunity for us to renew the covenant.

Read carefully the prophetic passage in Hosea and you will find references to God nurturing us. God teaches us to walk, takes us into God's loving arms, lifts us up for an embrace, and bends down and feeds us. God is fully involved in parenting. What a beautiful image of a God who nurtures us as one would nurture an infant!

Yet it was I who taught Ephraim to walk,
I took them up in my arms; . . .
I was to them like those who lift infants to their cheeks.
I bent down to them and fed them. (Hosea 11:3a, 4b)

Like a parent or like a nursery caregiver, God must discipline us for our own safety, growth, and protection. Yet, at the end of the Hosea passage, God, as Loving Parent, can no more give up on God's children than we could our own children. God offers forgiveness and an opportunity for the prodigal children to return.

How can I give you up, Ephraim?
How can I hand you over, O Israel? . . .
My heart recoils within me;
My compassion grows warm and tender. (Hosea 11:8)

Nurturing Infants

Newborns from birth to six weeks spend a lot of time sleeping—about twenty hours a day. This does not mean they will continually sleep for this amount of time. Babies will have periods of restlessness and times when they are alert. Newborns can recognize human voices, so in and out of these periods of sleeping they will begin to learn the voices of parents and caregivers. Nursery workers need to talk to babies in their care, using calming, affirming words. They can sing songs to the child about God as he or she is rocked to sleep. Talking to babies, singing to them, rocking them to sleep, and saying a prayer for them as they drift off for a nap are all ways to nurture infants.

Infants are sensory learners; they can see, hear, smell, and taste. Nursery workers should hold newborns close and soothe infants by the vibrations of their bodies. Sing to them or hum a song while holding them close. Mimic the sounds and facial expressions of the babies. All of these actions aid in the development of the child's sense of hearing and the sense of sight. Be sure the nursery has colorful mobiles, as these will also help infants with the senses of sight and sound. Make certain there are pleasant scents in the nursery room to stimulate the babies' sense of smell.

From *six week to five months*, babies will smile and laugh. They can begin to control their heads when on their backs. They learn to roll over from their back onto the stomach. During this age, infants are fascinated with their hands: staring at them, moving them, sucking on them, and wiggling them. They are also intrigued with sounds. Nursery workers should smile back at the baby and talk and laugh with infants. Church nurseries can place unbreakable mirrors so babies can watch themselves. Musical toys and brightly colored objects help develop the sense of sight and sound. Providing infants with many sensory experiences in the church nursery is one of the best ways to nurture infants.

The age of *five to eight months* is a period of developmental growth and change. Babies will double their birth weight by the age of six months, get their first tooth, and begin to sit up by themselves. They enjoy throwing, banging, and dropping objects. Provide toys in the nursery that help to stimulate babies in using the sense of touch. Remember that this is a time when babies learn to explore their environment. They enjoy dropping objects and having persons pick up the objects for them. Provide toys in the nursery that are age appropriate for infants. Remind nursery workers not to be frustrated if a child continues to throw his or her bottle, pacifier, or sippy cup. Be prepared for spills at this age. Nursery workers must remain calm and patient as these children explore the world around them. Also, remember that these children are beginning to cut teeth. A child that has usually been content in the nursery may now begin to cry and fuss. This baby will need extra rocking, soothing, and attention during the time he or she is cutting teeth.

By *eight months*, babies may show anxiety when a stranger comes into the nursery room. You notice that they cry and cling to the nursery worker most familiar to them. They may also cry when parents leave the nursery room. Nursery workers should take the crying child and assure parents that their child will be fine during their absence. Usually after a period of time the child will stop crying. Some parents will want to stay in the nursery until the child is calmed down. This is not a good idea. It disrupts the nursery setting. The child needs to learn that Mommy and Daddy will come back and that the nursery worker can be trusted. Assure parents that you can handle the situation and they need to leave and go to their class or to the worship service.

One of the reasons it is important to know exactly where parents are in your church building is in case you have to get them if a child will not stop crying and you are concerned. Trained nursery workers will know when to get parents. Most of the time it is best not to have to interrupt the parents, but there are times when it may be necessary to call parents to the nursery.

During these early months in an infant's life, the babies begin to enjoy playing games. One of the games they enjoy is to have an object hidden.

Nursery workers can ask, "Where did it go?" Then they can reveal the object to the child. Nursery workers can play Peek-a-Boo with these children. It is important to provide space in the nursery so these infants can kick, scoot, move freely, roll over, and crawl. Toys should be provided with different shapes. Silly games, safe age-level appropriate toys, and adequate space for play all help to nurture the nursery child.

Nursery workers can begin to talk with these infants about God. They can sing to the child and begin to use words that describe God as a loving God. They can also use words that affirm the child's worth. Workers might say, "I love you and God loves you" as they call the child by name. Music and short prayers can be used. Infants begin to pick up on words that are repeated over and over again, especially positive words about God, church, and themselves.

As an infant grows and is able to sit up, nursery workers need to be down on the floor playing and looking into the eyes and face of the child. This lets the child know that the caregivers really care about him or her and that they enjoying spending time with the child. This also communicates to the child that he or she is important to the nursery worker. We demonstrate this when we are willing to get down on the child's level.

Nursery workers can also point out pictures, placed at the eye level of the infant. These can be pictures of God's world or of children. Nursery workers can say, "See what a beautiful world God made." "See the pretty flower God made." "God loves you." Use encouraging words such as, "You are growing. Thank you God for helping us grow." Carry the child around the room pointing out pretty colors or different shapes. Infants begin to respond to their own names and will start to imitate sounds they hear from the caregivers in the church nursery.

From *eight to fourteen months*, babies are very active. They begin by scooting, crawling, and then walking. Nurseries must provide safe spaces for these babies to practice their crawling and walking.[1]

Nurturing Toddlers and Twos

Most toddlers and two-year-olds need a consistent routine. They do not like to have their schedules changed. There must be a regular routine in the nursery for these children so they will feel comfortable. Snack time, playtime, and story time should be at the same time each Sunday. These children also thrive on repetition. They like to hear the same Bible story, sing the same songs, and play the same games over and over.

Pray short prayers with these children, sing songs and read Bible stories about Jesus, God, church, and children. These stories should be short, keeping in mind the limited attention span of the toddler and twos. Toddlers and twos can learn that the Bible is a special book with many stories about God and Jesus. They can learn that God loves them. They can be taught that Jesus was a baby, just like them. Jesus had parents who loved him and helped him to grow. Toddlers and twos should learn from the nursery that church is a happy place. The nursery is one of the first places they learn to praise God. They praise God through listening to songs, through hearing prayers, and as they dance and clap their hands.

Teach toddlers and twos that the Bible is a special book. Have a place in the nursery room where the Bible is kept. From time to time, point out the Bible to the children and let them touch the Bible. Carry the Bible around the room and say, "This book is a special book. This is our Bible. It tells us about God and Jesus who love us."

Play is one of the most effective ways in which the toddler or two-year-old child learns. Nursery workers should play with children and allow them to interact with other children in the nursery. Be sure to choose toys that are age appropriate. Do not allow toys that are violent in nature such as play weapons. Blocks, dolls, puzzles, rhythm instruments, and other toys that help children use their imagination are good choices for the church nursery. Older nursery children enjoy role-playing toys and equipment where they can imitate adults. Through play, children model the adults in their lives. For example, a play kitchen sink, stove, and plastic dishes provide a way for children to pretend they are cooking and cleaning. These children also like playing on riding toys.

Children of this age need to have play experiences that help them express their creativity. They enjoy finger painting using shaving cream. They also like to draw and color. Keep in mind these children need jumbo crayons for their artwork. After children have completed their drawings, you may not be able to tell what they have drawn. When they approach you and say, "Look!" don't say, "What is that?" Ask the child to tell you about the picture. You nurture the nursery children when you allow them to draw or paint their own unique creations. Self-esteem is enhanced when the nursery workers compliment the children for their drawings or paintings. On the other hand, self-esteem can suffer when we ignore a child's artwork.

By the age of two, children will be able to better interact with one another. Two-year-olds still have difficulty sharing because they are still egocentric in nature and do not understand right from wrong. Be patient and loving with these children when they become frustrated, throw tantrums, and take another child's toy. Provide enough toys in the room so that all children have plenty of toys for playtime. Also, recognize that this age will probably prefer to play alone rather than with others.[2]

Discipline

Appropriate discipline in the church nursery depends on our understanding of developmental stages. The nursery worker must be able to decide which situations require discipline. Many potential disciplinary problems can be prevented when we have diligently planned the nursery environment so children have toys and space to explore. Yet when problems do occur, nursery workers need to be prepared. Workers should be trained in your church discipline policy, and your policy should be in writing for parents to read.

Help your workers to understand that discipline is not punishment. Discipline is an opportunity to teach children, to keep them safe, and to help them socialize with others. Young children learn self-control, self-help, and ways to get along with others through discipline. Learning and nurture occur when parents and teachers of infants, toddlers, or preschoolers set limits and encourage desired behavior.

Discipline for very young children is difficult. These nursery children are exploring and trying new things. They are too young to understand adult reasoning, but they do need limits to keep them safe. How you discipline children should depend on their age and developmental level.

Infants (birth-12 months) need a schedule for feeding, sleeping, and play. This will provide the infant with predictability, which will make them feel safe. For infants, it is not recommended that discipline come in the form of time-outs, as you might use with the toddler children. Time-out would only confuse an infant and hinder his or her trust in the nursery worker.

Early toddlers (one-two years) are beginning to explore their world. They may frustrate us and try our patience when they exercise their capability to use their own will against others. Discipline becomes necessary to ensure the child's safety, to stop aggression toward others, and to prevent destructive behavior. The best method is to remove the child from the situation and find another activity that is more suitable. For example, if you see a toddler starting to draw on the nursery wall, don't grab the crayon out of the child's hand. Instead, quickly give this child a piece of paper to draw on and remain with the child to affirm him or her when the child draws on the paper rather than the wall. Children of this age have a difficult time understanding verbal discipline, so it is best to redirect the child's behavior. Nursery workers will find it much easier to get a young child interested in something else than to take something away.

Besides redirecting a child's activity, nursery workers should keep breakable or dangerous items out of the reach of young children so they are not tempted. Sometimes we think that we can simply say to a child, "Don't pull my necklace" and the child will obey. Young children want to explore in order to learn. Touch is one way they do this. Put items you do not want children to touch out of reach so you will not have to worry about them being broken.

Find a safe way for children to be active. If a child starts throwing blocks while in the nursery, think about something he or she could safely throw. Say to the child, "It is not safe to throw the blocks. Someone could get hurt. Come here and throw these bean bags into the basket." Also, remember to reward children when they are playing nicely. Watch for the nursery children who are being good and reward them with a smile, hug, or word of praise. Let parents know when children have been especially good in the nursery.

Late toddlers (two-three years) are more temperamental. There will probably be more outbursts in the nursery as these children realize their limitations, yet struggle to be independent. Toddlers are still unsure how to express their frustration, and nursery workers must realize this and be patient and affirming. When a tantrum does occur, remove the child from the situation and environment in which the tantrum is happening. Redirect the activity and give the toddler some brief words of why the behavior is unacceptable. Always reassure the child of your love.

The job of a toddler is to taste, touch, smell, squeeze, poke, explore, and test. They do not share well. They need to assert themselves. One way they do this is to say "no" and not do what is asked of them.

Children three years and older can begin to accept limits, but they still need restrictions for their own safety. They need nursery workers to model good behavior for them. Consistency is a key when working with these children. "Time-out" may be used if the child loses control. Redirect the behavior, if possible. At this time in a child's life, praise and approval are the biggest motivators of good behavior.[3]

Criticizing, blaming, shaming, or using physical punishment should never be allowed in the nursery. Verbal abuse or physical punishment of any child would be grounds for dismissal of any nursery worker. Be sure that your nursery policy states clearly that you are not to use spanking or any physical force or restraint on the children.

One of the methods of discipline that many churches find effective is time-out. Time-out is not punishment. Time-out is intended to stop the action that may be hurting other children and give the child time to calm down. Hopefully, the child will realize that he or she has done something wrong and unacceptable.

Proponents of the time-out method suggest that one minute per year of age is sufficient time for the child in time-out. The nursery worker should not raise his or her voice when asking a child to go to time-out. They should talk to the child calmly, and give clear, simple directions. Use a firm, but friendly voice. Children can become overwhelmed with too many words and refuse to comply with your requests.

A small mat, small rug, or child-sized chair can be used for the time-out, but should be used only for this so as not to confuse children. Select an area of the nursery where you can see the child at all times.

Some child psychologists advocate using substitution activities such a having the child read a book or play with toys while in time-out. They believe that this helps the child calm down and redirect his or her negative activity to a positive one.

Time-out should only be used with behavior such as hitting, throwing objects, or biting. Churches should write into their discipline policies which behaviors warrant using time-out so nursery workers are clear about when to use it. Time-out should not be used for a child who is exploring the nursery and does not know he or she has done anything wrong. Some nursery workers have found it more effective to take a time-out with the child, especially those under three years of age. The nursery workers will take the child aside and share a calming activity with the child such as reading a book or talking quietly with the child.

Use methods of discipline that promote self worth. Let the child know that you understand what he or she is doing even if it is wrong behavior. The nursery worker might say, "Sally, I know you want to play with the doll, but Jessica is playing with it right now." This lets the child know that others have needs that must be respected. The worker can then say, "Soon, you can play with the doll." If you say this, follow through. One-year-olds understand when you say, "Just a minute" and will wait patiently as long as they do get to play with the doll a minute later. Two- and three-year olds can understand, "I will tell you when it is your turn to play with the doll." Follow through with your promise in about two or three minutes for the two- and three-year old children.

It is essential for churches to have a Safe Sanctuary policy. This policy examines issues related to child abuse in the church and offers ways to prevent any child being harmed. Included in your Safe Sanctuary policy should be discipline guidelines. Sometimes parents want you to adhere to the discipline policies they use in the home. If parents spank, they may give you permission to spank. You must communicate to parents that you cannot use this form of discipline in the church nursery. This is one of the reasons a discipline policy in writing is necessary. As you discipline children in the nursery you provide a safe environment for all children. This is another of the ways you nurture children.

Brain Development of Young Children

New studies into the brain development of infants provide helpful information for us as we work with children in the nursery. We are learning that the way we care for babies can aid or hinder his or her brain development. Within the first few months of life, babies' neurons, the "wiring" in the brain, develop rapidly. The babies' neurons develop 1,000 trillion connections, 20 times the number present at birth. The more connections there are, the better a child will be at learning, remembering, and carrying out tasks. From this we now understand that what we do to nurture a child in the first five years of life is decisive.[4]

How does all this apply to the church nursery? We must provide an environment where children are nurtured and cared for. We begin by paying attention to each baby. Watch the individual babies in your nursery as they move and play. By doing this, nursery workers can begin to learn what types of activities stimulate certain babies. They will learn what a certain child enjoys or does not like in the nursery environment. Nursery workers can be tempted to use restrictive devices such as cribs, playpens, highchairs, and swings. These should not be used too often and for great periods of time. Babies should be allowed opportunities to explore in a safe environment.

Nursery workers should be taught to respond when babies cry. Studies have shown that neglecting a crying baby can produce brain wave patterns that lessen happy feelings. A relaxed nursery worker will help the child to remain calm. Positive facial expressions communicate love and care.

A game such as Peek-a-Boo, counting games, and toys that help babies stack things, dump things out, and sort objects all help with brain development. So does the game of hiding objects and then asking, "Where did it go?" Nursery workers can place toys and objects around the room and let the babies explore. Look around your nursery to see if you have toys that stimulate children's imaginations.

Lighting in the nursery room can affect alertness and the way a child responds. Bright lights keep infants and toddlers alert. Soft lights will help infants and toddlers calm down. Colors can also stimulate the brain. Colors like pale yellow, beige, and off-white will create a calm learning environment. Bright colors such as red, orange, and yellow encourage creativity and excitement.

Researchers tell us that the ways we response to the nursery child's emotions are very important. When infants express positive or negative emotions, the caregiver should respond with sensitivity. When the caregiver responds with care and compassion, this action helps with early brain development. The shared emotion between a caregiver and a child, such as shared laughter and smiling, engages the child's brain activity in a positive way. The child develops a sense of security. Early brain research reinforces for us how important it is for nursery workers and others to be sensitive and responsive to infants' behavior and needs![5]

Curriculum

Curriculum in the church nursery is more than printed materials. Actually, it is the total experience that the child has in the nursery. For the infant, curriculum includes feeding, rocking, diapering, listening to music, hearing soothing words, and learning to trust. Provide a rocking chair or comfortable chair for the nursery workers to use to feed and rock babies to sleep. Safe swings and playpens should be purchased. A changing table should be clean. Beds and cribs should be checked for safety and clean sheets should be placed on the bed after each use. Toys and mobiles should be selected that will help nurture the senses of the infant.

For the toddler and twos, curriculum may include some printed material, such as a Bible picture card, but an important part of nursery curriculum may also include Bible stories, Bible songs, snack time, clean up time, and playtime. Play is one of the most essential elements of curriculum for the young child. We must choose toys, equipment, and materials that aid children in playtime rather than hinder their efforts to move around. Look in your nursery room and be sure that tables and equipment are the right size for the nursery children. Place pictures at the eye level of the child, not an adult's. Check to see that the nursery room is not too cluttered so children have adequate space to play. Place toys low enough that children can reach them to play and so they can help put toys away when playtime is over.

If your church nursery has space enough, set up some activity centers for toddlers and older nursery children. You might have a housekeeping area, a block area, a music area, and an art area. Provide books and puzzles that are age appropriate. Equipment, supplies, toys, books, puzzles, and learning centers in the nursery all help nurture the child.

What about printed curriculum? Can it be used in the church nursery? Toddlers and twos can benefit from a curriculum piece as long as the writers have taken into consideration the short attention span of the toddler and two-year-old. A Bible picture card is used by some denominations for these young children. One side of the card has a colorful picture, and the other side has a simple Bible story. The children take the Bible picture card home to be shared with the family. There is often a teacher book so that the toddler and twos teacher has guidelines on how to use the curriculum. Most teacher books provide thoughts on sharing the Bible lesson with the toddlers/twos, give ideas for crafts and snacks, suggest activities for the classroom, and list learning centers that can be set up in the room. Usually a music CD comes with the curriculum. This type of quality curriculum can greatly enhance the nurture of young children in your nursery.

Most denominations provide curriculum for children by the time they enter the three- and four-year-old Sunday school class. There will be a student book and teacher book as well as an activity packet and CD for music. Even if these age children are still a part of your nursery, you can provide curriculum for them. You nurture these children when you use curriculum that takes into account the developmental level of the children you teach.

What about special needs children in your church? Should you separate them from the other children? Should your nursery provide one-on-one care for these children who face physical or mental challenges? Some denominations now have curriculum designed for children who face physical or mental challenges. If you have enough children, you might consider establishing a class for them with a teacher who has been trained in caring for special needs children. You can also have a volunteer, perhaps a person who knows how to work with special needs children, to help the special needs child in the nursery. This one-on-one relationship might also apply to a child who has early onset of Attention Deficit Disorder, Bipolar Disorder, or any other children who may need special mentoring. You might have a list of persons who would rotate the task of working with the child. Be sure and train these volunteers. Whatever you decide to do, consult with the parents and be sure these children are not singled out as problem children.

Suggestions on Ways to Nurture Children in the Nursery

1. Talk to babies. Mimic the sounds and facial expressions of babies.
2. Sing to babies. Sing songs about God, Jesus, and the Church.
3. Sooth babies by holding them close so they can feel the vibrations of the caregiver's body.
4. Respond when babies cry.
5. Pray simple prayers with and for nursery children.
6. Provide ways for infants to use their senses.
7. Play CDs with songs about God, Jesus, and the church.
8. Provide space in the nursery room for children to explore.
9. Play games such as Peek-a-Boo and counting games.
10. Talk with infants about God. Say, "I love you," and, "God loves you."
11. Affirm the self-worth of each child. Say, "You are growing!" "You are so pretty!" "You are so loved."
12. Place pictures in the church nursery at the eye level of children.
13. Let toddlers and twos dance to music.
14. Place the Bible in a special spot in the nursery room. Hold the Bible and let children touch it. Say, "This is a special book about God and Jesus."
15. Get down on the floor and play with children.
16. Use positive and affirming discipline.
17. Provide a routine in the toddler room.
18. Recognize the importance of repetition for the toddler. Repeat stories and songs.
19. Provide quality printed curriculum for the toddler age and above.
20. Understand the importance of colors used in the nursery.
21. Set up activity/learning centers for older nursery children.
22. Allow nursery children to be creative with artwork.
23. Provide separate room for infants from older nursery children. As your nursery grows, provide rooms to adequately accommodate various ages of nursery children.
24. Understand the short attention span of nursery children.
25. Provide toys, puzzles, and books that are age appropriate.
26. Partner with the home in faith formation. Provide materials that help parents teach children in the faith.

Extending Nursery Nurture Principles to Other Parts of the Church

As God nurtures us, we must nurture all of God's children in our congregations, regardless of their ages. Is yours a nurturing church that follows the example of a nurturing God?

We learn from the nursery the importance of being taught in an environment that is calming and affirming. Walk around your church and take a look at the classrooms for children, youth, and adults. Is there enough space to do the activities needed for a particular age group? Is each classroom stocked with proper supplies for the age meeting in the classroom? Is the furniture the correct scale and size for the age of the learner? The environment of the classroom can hinder or help in the nurture of children, youth, and adults.

As children leave the nursery and continue their faith journey, they, too, should be provided with a calming and affirming atmosphere. Teachers who are patient with children should be chosen to work in Sunday school, Vacation Bible school, and other areas of children's ministry. Never let persons work with children who have a harsh temper or easily become stressed out around children. A relaxed, pleasant environment will nurture children, whereas a stressed, hectic environment can hinder the nurture of children.

The same principle applies to our youth and adults. Youth can easily pick up signals from teachers who are stressed. They never want to be embarrassed or singled out by a leader. Select persons to nurture youth who are easy going, yet committed, mature leaders. Youth want to be treated as teenagers and not children. Youth are nurtured when they have activities and Bible lessons that meet their needs and are relevant to their lifestyles. Allow youth to express their opinions and share their concerns. Our youth have been raised in a technological age. Often when they come to Sunday school, they come to rooms that look like they were designed for learning that is not relevant for today's youth. Churches can nurture youth by providing a space for learning that is appealing to them. Bible computer programs could be used to enhance a Bible lesson. Movie clips and Christian music can nurture youth.

Adults also need leaders who do not bring their own problems into the classroom. Adults are nurtured in an environment where they are affirmed and where they can relax and not have to put on pretenses.

People of all ages in our church need Bible stories and lessons that are appropriate for their age and developmental level. Children are nurtured best when teachers use vocabulary words that children understand, when they share Bible stories that are geared for the age level of the child, and when they share activities and crafts that children can apply to the Bible lesson. Teachers must realize that all children do not learn in the same way. Some children are visual learners. Others enjoy moving their bodies as they play games or sway to music. Train children's teachers in the different ways children can learn.

A good resource is to take a look at the theory of multiple intelligences proposed by Howard Gardner, an educator who identified several ways persons learn. Gardner, a Harvard University psychology professor, challenged the widely held notion that we all learn in the same way. Some of us, he proposed, are verbal learners. We learn best through words, such as hearing Bible stories. Others, he observed learn through visuals, by looking at pictures, movies, or seeing objects. Some children learn most effectively through the application of mathematical skills so they might enjoy problem solving or deciphering codes. Still others enjoy learning through listening to music or singing. You might discover that some of your students need physical movement in the classroom. They thrive on learning through games, dance, and role-play.[6] Gardner believed that most students needed to use one or more of these methods for positive learning. Understanding ways children learn will help us to nurture them.

Selecting good quality curriculum can nurture persons in your church. Take a careful look at the curriculum your children, youth, and adult classes are using. A curriculum committee can be formed to make decisions on what curriculum classes are to use. Many churches have a policy that states that children and youth classes must use curriculum from their own denomination's resources. Adults might have the option of selecting their own curriculum, but only after approval by the curriculum committee. Whatever policy you develop, be sure your congregation understands the importance of curriculum as a tool to nurture all ages in your church.

Children are often nurtured by learning centers that are suggested in their curriculum. Some churches are using a rotation model with their children in Sunday school. In the rotation model, children study the same lesson for several weeks, but are able to visit a learning center each week that helps them apply the lesson. One church recently remodeled the children's classrooms and developed a snack room, craft room, and Bible lesson room. Children visit each of these rooms during their Sunday school time. Keep in mind that youth and adults often enjoy learning centers, particularly for special events in your church such as an intergenerational Advent event where all ages might move from one center to another.

Just as we limit the use of anything in the nursery that would hinder an infant's ability to explore and learn, we do not want to place limits on the ability of any of our age-levels in the church to engage in spiritual growth. Children should be allowed to ask questions, play Bible games, participate in mission activities, and engage in activities that stimulate their minds and bodies.

Youth should have opportunities to probe into faith matters with supportive adults. Your church should be a place where youth do not feel restricted to search, question, and seek answers to the tough decisions of life and faith. Youth should be given opportunities to share their faith and participate in mission activities.

Adults should also find your church a place where they are invited to come as they are without restrictions. Some adults do not always feel welcome to come to our churches. Strive to remove any barriers that would keep adults from being welcomed and nurtured in the faith.

For all ages, faith is nurtured in an environment where persons are not restricted in the way they explore their faith, but persons are heard and their questions are answered in an honest manner.

Ways Churches Can Nurture

1. Select teachers and leaders who demonstrate a calming, positive, affirming manner as they work with persons.
2. Train teachers and leaders in sharing age-appropriate Bible stories.
3. Train teachers and leaders in sharing age-appropriate vocabulary.
4. Place pictures at the eye-level of the students.
5. Check lighting in the classrooms.
6. Select colors for the classrooms. Use soothing colors in parts of the room that will be calming. Use bold, vibrant colors to stimulate students.
7. Provide adequate space in classrooms according to the age-level of students.
8. Provide teachers training in the way persons learn. Teach about Howard Gardner's multiple intelligences. Many denominational curriculum list Gardner's theory as a part of teacher introductory material. More detailed information is found in Howard Gardner's book *Frames of Mind: The Theory of Multiple Intelligences.*
9. Use learning centers in the classrooms or for special events.

10. Use the rotation model for children. If you do not want to use it year-round, experiment with this method during the summer months.
11. Provide all classes with quality curriculum.
12. Partner with the home in providing resources to nurture families.
13. Use positive discipline methods that are not viewed as punishment.
14. Establish a Safe Sanctuary policy and train all volunteers who work with children and youth. Resources: *Safe Sanctuaries: Reducing the Risk of Child Abuse in the Church,* Joy Thornburg Melton; *Safe Sanctuaries: Reducing the Risk of Abuse in Youth Ministries,* Joy Thornburg Melton
15. Allow students to ask questions and explore faith in an unrestricted environment.
16. If you have special needs children, youth, or adults, check to see if your denomination has resources for teaching and nurturing those with physical and mental challenges.

Chapter Four Endnotes

1. Mary Jane Pierce Norton, "Infants, Toddlers, and Twos-Watch Them Grow!" in *The First Three Years: A Guide for Ministry with Infants, Toddlers & Two-Year-Olds,* ed. Mary Alice Gran (Nashville: Discipleship Resources, 1989), 16.
2. Mary Jane Pierce Norton, "Helping the Young Child Grow in Faith," in *The First Three Years: A Guide for Ministry with Infants, Toddlers & Two-Year-Olds,* ed. Mary Alice Gran (Nashville: Discipleship Resources, 1989), 27.
3. Campbell, Tanya. "Discipling Your Children, Infants & Toddlers." suite 101.com 24 May, 2007. 14 Aug. 2008 [http://www.infantstoddlers.suite101.com/article.cfm/disciplining_your_children].
4. Barrett, K. C., Gains, S., Jacobson, B. "Helping Babies Learn." Colorado State University Extension. 11 July, 2008. 14 Aug. 2008. [http://www.ext.colostate.edu/PUBS/consumer/10220.html].
5. Gable, Sara. "Nature, Nurture, & Early Brain Development." University of Missouri Extension. August, 2001. 14 Aug. 2008. [http://www.extension.missouri.edu/xplor/hesguide/humanrel/gh6115.htm].
6. Gardner, Howard, *Frames of Mind: The Theory of Multiple Intelligences* (New York: Basic Books, 1983), 73-205.

Chapter Five

LULLABY AND GOOD NIGHT

Resting in God's Grace

Betty and Mike are excitedly and joyfully expecting their first child, a girl they plan to name Allison. Betty has spent months preparing the nursery room at their home. She has painted the walls, purchased nursery furniture, and decorated the room with a colorful mobile and cheerful pictures. She has read numerous books on childcare and parenting. Her husband Mike has already invested in a college fund for his child because Mike strongly believes in preparing well ahead of time for the future. Allison's grandmother has stepped in and volunteered to keep the baby while Betty and Mike are at work. Betty and Mike have toured the infant room in their church nursery, met the nursery caregiver, and taken the time to talk with their pastor about infant baptism. In a sense they have gone ahead of their unborn child to prepare the way for this child to be received in a loving and welcoming environment. Parents, grandparent, and Allison's congregation are already at work in the life of this unborn child, even if the child is unaware of their efforts.

Yet these individuals are not the only ones who are reaching out to this child before her birth. God has already been at work in the life of Allison, extending to her grace and love. God has claimed Allison as God's child and has begun to work in her life. Of course Allison has no idea that God is reaching out to her. She is not even born! However, this fact does not stop God from seeking her as God's own. The work that God has begun in the life of Allison will continue throughout her life, even in the times in which Allison will turn away from God. God will constantly woo Allison, seeking to bring her back into a relationship with her Maker. This is a gracious offering from God to Allison and there is nothing Allison can ever do to earn this unmerited gift. In time, she will realize she can only receive it.

The Role of Grace

Those of us in the Wesleyan heritage recognize that this God-initiated care is what is known as *prevenient* grace. John Wesley, the founder of the people called Methodists, believed that God marked each child with the gift of grace. A child who experienced nurture in a Christian home and congregation would later come to justifying grace, whereupon the child accepts for himself or herself the work of God. The individual then begins the journey of sanctification, a process of growth and perfection in the Christian faith.

As we consider our work with children, especially nursery children, we might think of this grace as preparing grace. We are extending love and grace in ways that will prepare our children to become aware of God's love. We are preparing each to respond to the love of God in Jesus Christ.

Your church nursery is full of prevenient grace! Your nursery room is overflowing with grace upon grace! Here is a place where God is at work reaching out to your infants prior to their awareness of God. Our understanding of God's grace provides a powerful model for us of the ways in which we should practice grace in the nursery as well as how we demonstrate grace to the parents of nursery children.

Include in your nursery training a session on grace as taught in our Wesleyan tradition. Give nursery caregivers a simple definition of prevenient grace and provide some biblical examples. Included in this chapter are some statements about prevenient grace as well as some Scriptures you might use in your training workshop. You can also give these statements and Scriptures to nursery parents to help them better understand God's grace at work in the life of their child. Helping your nursery caregivers grasp this important concept in our Wesleyan tradition will not only shape the way they extend grace in the nursery, but will also help them to understand infant baptism as well. Your parents will also have a better understanding of infant baptism and realize how closely it is tied to our understanding of grace. Parents and congregation can more faithfully fulfill their role as nurturers of the faith of children when they have a greater appreciation of the gift of God's grace.

Congregations that baptize infants approach this sacrament from their belief in God's grace, in particular prevenient grace. We believe that God reaches out to the child in baptism, claiming the child as God's own and marking the child with God's grace. Later, the baptized child nurtured in the home by believing parents and raised in a congregation of faith will accept for himself or herself the grace of God. The child will confirm what the parents and congregation did for the child at his or her baptism. At the baptism of a child, believing parents and congregation vow to raise the child in the Christian faith. Nursery caregivers need to realize that they have an essential part to play in the upholding of this vow.

The Gift of Grace

Your church nursery may be a welcoming place where nursery caregivers know the names of your children and provide them quality care. Your nursery could be equipped with everything that is needed and recommended to make your nursery environment of the highest caliber. You might pride yourself on the excellent job your nursery workers do in nurturing children in the faith. However, if you do not extend grace you will be missing out on offering one of the greatest gifts you can give your nursery children and parents. How can we offer the gift of grace in our church nursery? Let us examine some of the ways our church nurseries can be places of grace. We discover that our understanding and practice of grace have implications for the faith journey of our nursery children and their parents.

God reaches out and claims us before we are aware of God's love. We must do the same for the children God places in our church nursery. Even before a child is born, we can begin to make preparations to welcome this child to the church nursery. We can reach out to the parents and make certain they know that the child is going to be welcomed into a loving, caring environment. Not all of your expectant parents will reach out to the church nursery by asking for information or seeking to tour your nursery. Therefore, leaders in the church should make sure that there is a person in contact with the expectant parents to give them information about the nursery or to check on the progress of the pregnancy. This might be a layperson selected as your nursery home visitor, a member of the children's committee, a nursery caregiver, or a pastor in the church. By reaching out to the family before a child is even born and becoming involved in the life of this child, you demonstrate the grace of God that reaches out to us before we are born and before we are aware of this grace. You claim this child as your own even before his or her birth.

God's grace is a gift. There is absolutely nothing we can do to earn this free offering given to us by God. When you offer love, welcome, and care to the nursery children, you do so knowing that they can do nothing to earn your hospitality. As yet, they are not able to use their gifts to share with the church. They are not at the point where they are able to make a monetary contribution to your congregation. All they can share with you are their cries, their laughter, their hugs, and their needs. When you make the children in the nursery a priority for your church you are extending God's grace. You are modeling an example of grace that cannot be earned, but that is given out of love.

This is a powerful lesson for your church. Often we are willing to reach out to those who can do something for us. We are glad to extend hospitality to those who have much to offer our church. Are we willing to reach out to those who can give very little to us, but are in great need? By providing care for the nursery children simply out of love and grace you teach the entire church a powerful lesson in God's grace given to us as a free gift.

Extending Grace

Nursery caregivers may find it easier to extend grace to some children than others. Our temptation is to extend grace to those who are easy to love and pleasant to be around. God does not pick and choose who receives the gift of grace. God's grace is offered freely to all of God's children. In the nursery, we must be careful not to exclude any child from receiving our grace and love. Some children make our tasks in the nursery enjoyable. They are easy-going babies who rarely fuss and delight us with their smiles and cooing sounds. Other babies are constantly fussy and in demand of our attention. Some babies are slow in developmental tasks and may try our patience in the nursery. We may minister to some babies who have physical or mental challenges. Grace must be extended to all.

Nursery caregivers should be especially careful not to play favorites when it comes to the nursery children. Our aim ought to be to treat all children with respect and give each child the same amount of love, care, and attention. This is especially important when dealing with children who are different from what some might consider the nursery norm. Never let cultural differences keep you from extending God's grace. Never allow negative feelings toward any child keep you from showing the grace of God. Demonstrating God's grace in the midst of a difficult situation or a tiring day in the nursery when a certain child strains our nurturing skills is challenging. Yet we strive to show that God's grace and our grace is for all of the children, not just a select few.

Like our nursery children, there are some parents who are easier to work with than others. Some parents of nursery children make our tasks rewarding and others may stretch us in our ability to extend God's grace. There are always those parents who do everything you request of them. They mark the child's belongings, they bring adequate bottles and diapers, they thank you and show appreciation for your work, and they always arrive on time to pick up their infant. How easily we can shower grace upon these parents!

Grace and Discipline

What about those parents who never follow the nursery rules? They are always late, causing volunteers to have to wait before they can leave the nursery. They forget to bring a bottle, leaving you in a dilemma when it comes to feeding time. They never seem to have enough diapers in their child's diaper bag. Extending grace to these parents shows that we understand God's grace that reaches out to us when we act undeservingly. You never know what these parents are facing in their homes or personal lives. There may be some situations of which you are unaware where these parents need an extra dose of grace. While you do not want to break the nursery rules for these parents, try to go out of your way to work with them as best you can. Gently remind them of the nursery rules and extend grace at times in spite of the rules.

Caregivers may encounter situations which make the decision to bend or enforce the rules very difficult. There may be times in which you will need to consult with your pastors or children's ministry committee to seek advice. Take for example a situation where a child has reached the age to move out of the nursery to the preschool children's area. Yet, each week the parents continue to bring the child into the nursery. Do you extend grace or do you enforce your nursery rule that states that at a certain age children are to graduate from the nursery to the preschool area?

Talk with these parents of the child openly and honestly. Explain to them the ages of nursery children in your church that is stated in your nursery policy. That is why it is essential to have a written nursery policy to refer to in these situations. Find out why the parents insist on continuing to leave the child in the nursery. You will then need to decide whether to extend grace to this family. Sometimes you extend grace to a family by asking them to follow your rules because this benefits all of the families in your nursery area. You extend grace to all the nursery children by removing a child who is too old for the nursery and poses a problem in terms of safety for the other children. Each situation is different, and there are some times in which you have to err on the side of grace. Pray for God's grace for your caregivers and for your nursery families in these difficult situations in the church nursery.

Affirming Grace in the Nursery

Children begin their faith journey at your church in the nursery, so here will be one of the first places where children have the opportunity to experience grace. Caregivers are pivotal persons who help children grow in faith. They teach children about a God of grace and, like God, they themselves are givers of grace. Caregivers are partners with God in the good work that God is doing in the lives of the nursery children. What an awesome responsibility and privilege!

As we nurture children in the nursery we affirm the creative work that God is doing in the life of each child. We desire to start each nursery child out on a faith journey that is positive. We want to do all we can to help these children discover God's purpose for their lives. We do this as we guide them in the right direction from the very beginning of life. We nurture the grace that is evident in each child. We watch with joyful anticipation as children grow and develop and come to know a God of grace. We ourselves must be grace-givers who help our infants and toddlers discover that God has a unique plan for each child.

When we confirm God's grace in the lives of our nursery children, we proclaim that we trust in a God who is beginning a good work in the lives of our infants. God has a purpose for each child. We rejoice because we know that God designed wonderful plans for the infants that we care for in our church nursery. Nursery caregivers are workers with God to help shape infants and help mold them into the persons that God desires them to become. Pray each day for the children and parents you work with that God's plan and purpose will be accomplished in the lives of the nursery children and their families. You may not see this plan fully realized, because the child will leave the nursery and hopefully will eventually grow into adulthood. Yet you have planted seeds of grace that you trust will grow and mature in the years to come.

We believe that God's grace continues to work throughout the life journey. Yet our first understanding of God's grace comes to us as infants. In our Wesleyan understanding of grace, we believe that God works so powerfully in our lives that we are moved toward God's grace. John Wesley believed that God was always prompting us to respond to God's grace. God creates within us the desire to know God. We are drawn to God by God's very act of loving us, thus causing us to want to be in relationship with God.

As God is working in the life of the nursery child, nursery caregivers are also working to extend grace and to show the love of God to the infants in their care. God continues to love and care for us all of our lives. How wonderful to begin our faith journey in the church in an environment where grace is extended to us by loving, caring persons. In a powerful sense, we cooperate with God's movement of grace in the child's life when we do all we can to extend God's grace in the church nursery. When we nurture children in the faith, we help to prompt them toward a desire to know a God of grace. We spark an interest in the child in knowing a God who meets his or her every need because we have met their needs and shown them grace upon grace each time they are brought to the church nursery.

Wesley believed that there would come a time in every person's life when he or she would have to accept God's grace. Our decision to follow God and say "yes" to Christ was what Wesley called *justifying* grace. Our task in the church nursery is to nurture children in the faith in anticipation of that time when God's justifying grace will be evident in the life of each child. We nurture them in confidence and trust that they will accept God's grace for themselves and profess their faith in Christ. Our task in the church nursery is vitally important when we realize that we are preparing children to move toward God's justifying grace.

As you work with nursery children, realize that they are individuals with their own free will. Do all you can to start them out on a strong faith journey, but realize that they must make their own decisions to turn to God or to reject God. Pray for children on their faith journey because we know that all of them will stumble and fall at times. Pray that they will accept God's grace offered to them in Jesus Christ. Realize, though, that we must leave the results up to God and the work of the Holy Spirit.

God's grace protects us, guides us, convicts us of sin, and imparts to us the desire and ability to repent and to come to faith in Jesus Christ. We desire this for each of our nursery children as they grow and mature in faith.

While our children do not belong to us, but to God, we *have* been entrusted with their care and nurture. God's grace is sufficient to meet the needs of each child. God's grace is abundant. God's grace never runs out. Our God is a "God of all grace." In response to God's grace given to each of us, we are called by God to extend grace to others.

You have a checklist of items to be included in your church nursery, do you not? Among these essential items are cribs, swings, mobiles, diaper pails, books, puzzles, toys, diapers, wipes, clean sheets, and a myriad of other necessities to make your nursery an excellent place for the care of children. Should you not put grace at the top of your list? If you do not have it there, for the sake of each nursery child, put it there now. Then practice it in such a way that it cannot be contained in your nursery room, but overflows to all areas of your church life. What greater gift can you share with your nursery children and your entire congregation than God's free, abounding gift of grace?

Dealing with a Difficult Situation

Grace and Death of a Child

What happens if your church experiences the untimely death of one of your nursery children and this child has not been baptized? Grieving parents need to experience the gift of grace from their congregation and nursery workers at this difficult time. They also want the assurance that baptism is not absolutely necessary for salvation. An infant who dies without the sacrament of baptism is under God's prevenient grace. God loves and cares for this child and will extend grace to the child. Assure your parents that God's grace is at work. Demonstrate this grace by reaching out to the family providing meals and comforting them in every way possible.

It is easy to get so busy ministering to the parents of a child who has died that we forget about the other siblings in the family. They, too, are grieving. Go out of your way to extend grace and love to other children in the family. Children will often feel that they have done something to cause the death of a family member. Assure these children that they did not do anything to cause the death of the infant. If, however, another child in the family has contributed in any way to the child's death, extend grace to this hurting child and help the family find counseling for the child.

Parents of an infant who has died may feel guilt and uncertainty because they did not have their child baptized. While the sacrament of baptism is a powerful demonstration of God's grace at work in the life of a child, an infant who dies without being baptized is loved and cared for by God just as much as the baptized infant.[1]

Suggestions on How to Discuss Prevenient Grace with Nursery Workers, Parents, and Congregation.

1. Grace is God's unmerited love offered to us as a gift. Grace is a free gift and there is nothing we can do to earn it.
2. Prevenient grace is God's grace offered to us before we are even aware of God's presence in our life.
3. Prevenient grace is preparing grace. We are extending grace to our children so that will be prepared to receive God's love and grace. We are preparing them to respond to God in their lives.
4. Prevenient or preventing grace means, "coming before" or "preceding." God goes before us to offer grace and prepare us to accept God's love for us.
5. Prevenient grace draws us toward God and toward faith in Jesus Christ. We are able to respond to God and Christ in faith because prevenient grace sparks in us an interest in the Christian life.
6. Prevenient grace is present with us throughout our life journey. God never gives up on us, but is always seeking a relationship with God's children.
7. Prevenient grace works in our lives when we stray from God or reject God. There is no place or point in our life in which God gives up on us. God is constantly seeking us.
8. John Wesley trusted that as God's prevenient grace worked in the life of an individual, that person would come to accept for himself or herself God's grace. Wesley called this decision to turn to God, to say "yes" to Jesus Christ, as justifying grace. The individual then begins a faith journey of growth which Wesley called sanctification. Wesley believed in free will, so the individual could "fall from grace" when he or she turned away from God and chose a life of sin.
9. Prevenient grace is evident at the baptism of a child. Infant baptism is seen as a celebration of prevenient grace. This is one of the reasons we practice infant baptism. Although infant baptism is important, it is not essential.
10. Prevenient grace is evident when a child dies, even if this child has not been baptized. God's grace extends to this child in just as powerful a way as to any other child.
11. All persons are under God's prevenient grace. God does not choose some to receive this grace and reject others from receiving God's gift of grace.

12. We see prevenient grace at work in our lives when God protects us, guides us, convicts us of sin, gives us the desire and ability to repent of our sins, and leads us to a relationship with Jesus Christ.
13. The Holy Spirit plays a role in prevenient grace. The work of the Holy Spirit is to bring us to an awareness of our sin and our need for God's forgiveness. The Holy Spirit guides us to accept God's prevenient grace in our lives.
14. God's grace is abundant. It never runs out.
15. God's grace is sufficient to meet all of our needs regardless of our situations and problems in life.
16. God's grace should lead us to be thankful and to extend grace to others.
17. Prevenient grace affirms our belief that Christ died for all persons. Christ died for the sins of the entire world and not an elected few.
18. The Fall is a term that refers to original sin as depicted in the Bible story of Adam and Eve. John Wesley believed that in the fall of humanity, we did not totally lose our creation in the image of God. God had placed a small spark of divine grace in each of us. We are thus able to receive God's prevenient grace; that then leads us to justifying and sanctifying grace.
19. Often we are unaware of God's prevenient grace at work in our lives at the moment it is happening. Many times we look back at events in our lives and recognize that God's prevenient grace was working even if we were not aware of it at the time. Our failure to recognize or acknowledge God's prevenient grace does not make it any less powerful or effective in our lives.
20. No matter how far we get from God's grace it is never to late to return to God and receive God's grace.
21. Prevenient grace is a crucial element in the Wesleyan theology of childhood. Prevenient grace draws the child toward God and to the love of Christ.

Scriptural Support of Prevenient Grace

Before I formed you in the womb I knew you, and before you were born I consecrated you; I appointed you a prophet to the nations. (Jeremiah 1:5) God's prevenient grace is at work in the life of Jeremiah. God knows Jeremiah even before he is born. God has a special purpose for Jeremiah. In the same way, God knows each of us and has a plan for our life.

But when God, who had set me apart before I was born and called me through his grace . . . . (Galatians 1:15) The Apostle Paul is called by God to preach the gospel. He was called and set apart before he was even born. God's prevenient grace is evident in the life of Paul as it is in the life of each of us.

When Israel was a child, I loved him, . . .Yet it was I who taught Ephraim to walk, I took them up in my arms; but they did not know that I healed them. I led them with cords of human kindness, with bands of love. I was to them like those who lift infants to their cheeks. I bent down to them and fed them. (Hosea 11:1a, 3-4) Here is one of the most moving passages in all of Scripture. Hosea presents a picture of a Parenting God. God extends grace to the children of Israel even when they are unfaithful. Israel is portrayed as an infant whom God feeds, comforts, and teaches to walk. God's prevenient grace is given to each of us and God protects, comforts, and teaches us like those "infants" in the Hosea passage.

For thus says the Lord God: I myself will search for my sheep, and will seek them out. (Ezekiel 34:11) God's prevenient grace seeks us out.

For by grace you have been saved through faith, and this is not your own doing; it is the gift of God. (Ephesians 2:8) Grace is God's free gift to us. There is not anything we can do to earn God's grace or our salvation.

"They are now justified by his grace as a gift, through the redemption that is in Christ Jesus." (Romans 3:24) In this passage, Paul assures us that grace is a gift, which leads to justifying grace when we enter into a relationship with Christ.

Therefore, to keep me from being too elated, a thorn was given to me in the flesh, a messenger of Satan to torment me, to keep me from being too elated. Three times I appealed to the Lord about this, that it would leave me, but he said to me, "My grace is sufficient for you, for power is made perfect in weakness."
(2 Corinthians 12:7b-9a) The Apostle Paul asserts with great confidence that God's grace is sufficient to meet our needs even when situations are difficult.

He was a devout man who feared God with all his household; he
gave alms generously to the people and prayed constantly to God.
One afternoon at about three o'clock he had a vision in which he
clearly saw an angel of God coming in and saying to him,
"Cornelius." He stared at him in terror and said, "What is it, Lord?"
He answered, "Your prayers and your alms have ascended as a
memorial before God. Now send men to Joppa for a certain Simon
who is called Peter; he is lodging with Simon, a tanner, whose house
is by the seaside." When the angel who spoke to him had left, he
called two of his slaves and a devout soldier from the ranks of those
who served him, and after telling them everything, he sent them to
Joppa. (Acts 10:2-8) Read Acts 10:1-44. This is the story of Peter
and Cornelius. Cornelius is not a follower of Christ, but he is a
devout man who gives money to the poor. God begins to work in the
life of Cornelius guiding him to the moment in which he would meet
Peter and then he would decide to become a follower of Christ. God
was working in the life of Cornelius before his conversion by offering him prevenient grace. The Holy Spirit was preparing Cornelius
to receive Peter and his gospel message.

Now when they heard this, they were cut to the heart and said to
Peter and to the other apostles, "Brothers, what should we do?"
(Acts 2:37) Read Acts 2:1-41. On the day of Pentecost, thousands of
people were gathered in the city of Jerusalem. God's prevenient
grace, through the empowering of the Holy Spirit, worked in the
hearts of these persons to lead them to salvation in Christ.

A certain woman named Lydia, a worshipper of God, was listening
to us; she was from the city of Thyatira and a dealer in purple cloth.
The Lord opened her heart to listen eagerly to what was said by
Paul. (Acts 16:14) Read Acts 16:11-15. Lydia's life was greatly
affected by prevenient grace. Prevenient grace went before Lydia,
preparing her to receive Paul when he arrived in her community.

Then he brought them outside and said, "Sirs, what must I do to be
saved?"(Acts 16:30) Read Acts 16:16-34. The preaching and singing
of Paul and Silas moved the Philippian jailer. The jailer was convicted of his sins by God's prevenient grace, but he recognizes that
he has a further need of salvation. He asks to be baptized and
accepts God's justifying grace in his life. Notice that his entire family

is baptized. Surely some of these family members baptized that day were infants.

You who want to be justified by the law have cut yourselves off from Christ; you have fallen away from grace. (Galatians 5:4) Wesley believed that we could fall from grace as indicated by this Scripture.

But grow in the grace and knowledge of our Lord and Savior Jesus Christ. To him the glory both now and to the day of eternity. Amen. (2 Peter 3:18) Our salvation is a journey and we must grow in God's grace.

You then, my child, be strong in the grace that is in Christ Jesus. (2 Timothy 2:1) Timothy is encouraged to remain strong in the grace extended to him by Jesus Christ.

No one can come to me unless drawn by the Father who sent me; and I will raise that person up on the last day. (John 6:44) God's prevenient grace draws us toward God and Christ.

He has shown you, O man, what is good . . . (Micah 6:8a) John Wesley interprets Micah 6:8 as an example of prevenient grace. God's Spirit reveals to us what is good.

Suppose one of you has a hundred sheep and loses one of them. Does he not leave the ninety-nine in the open country and go after the lost sheep until he finds it? (Luke 15:4) Read Luke 15:1-7. This Scripture is known as the Parable of the Lost Sheep. God is portrayed as a shepherd who searches out the lost sheep. God searches for us with prevenient grace when we stray from God.

Prevenient Grace at Work in the Life of the Congregation

God's prevenient grace reaches out and claims us before we are even aware that God is at work in our lives. God's prevenient grace is already at work in our lives from the moment we are born. We have claimed this promise for our nursery children, but do we see it as a reality in the lives of others in our congregation? Persons in our churches need time to reflect on the ways in which they have sensed God working in their lives. Often, it is only when we look back at certain circumstances in our lives that we realize God was present. As we remember a particular situation, we now recognize God was offering us prevenient grace even though at the time we were unaware of God's action. Give persons opportunities in small groups, Sunday school, or your worship time to testify to God's grace at work in their lives. Share sermons and Bible studies centered on God's prevenient, justifying, and sanctifying grace.

Churches that teach prevenient grace should do all in their power to love and nurture the children in the congregation. We are all responsible for our children and their faith journey. All of the members of the congregation should be concerned that children are being guided toward God's justifying grace. We cannot make the decision for our children, but we strive to see that they have the best teachers to model the Christian faith. Children need many well-planned experiences to help them grow and mature so they can come to the decision to say 'yes" to God's grace for themselves. Pastors and leaders responsible for confirmation classes or discipleship classes for children and youth should be sure these classes are excellent. When a child or youth does profess faith in Christ and accept God's justifying grace, we should rejoice with the child and youth and continue to affirm God's prevenient, justifying, and sanctifying grace.

Chapter Five Endnotes

1. McAnally, Thomas S., *Questions and Answers About the United Methodist Church* (Nashville: Abingdon Press, 1995), 7.

Chapter Six

PASS IT ON

Volunteers in the Nursery & Family of God

One-year-old Aaron was born into a large family household in a small village in ancient Israel. While his father and brothers are working in the field, his mother, his grandmother, and his two sisters care for Aaron. When his mother and sisters must help his father and brothers harvest the grapes from their meager vineyard, he is watched over by his doting grandfather who tells him stories of the history of his people. His grandmother sings to him the ancient songs of the Hebrew faith as she rocks him to sleep. Aaron's family and community include him in the Jewish festivals. His senses awaken to the sounds of poems and scriptures recited aloud by leaders of his village. He mimics the laughter of the elders as they share humorous tales of past adventures. He sees the tears and hears the sorrow in the voices of his elders as they recall the tragic events of their tradition.

As the past history of his people is recounted, Aaron wiggles in the arms of his mother or falls asleep to the soothing voices of his community singing praises to God. Even as an infant Aaron senses that he is an important child of God. Born and raised in an intergenerational environment, Aaron is blessed to be a part of a community where he is nurtured by several generations of relatives and friends.

One-year-old Sophia was born into a Christian family in the city of Cenchreae. Her family worships in the home of Phoebe, a deacon and hostess of the household church that meets weekly. Sophia received the sacrament of infant baptism, celebrated by her parents, her brothers, her sister, deacon Phoebe, and members of the household church. Sophia's senses awaken to the sounds of hymns sung, prayers recited, meals shared, and stories told of a man named Jesus. She loves to come to Phoebe's house church because here she gets lots of attention from persons of different generations. Sister Mary, a devout member of the church, holds her during worship. Older children play "peek-a-boo." An elder and leader in the church named John smiles and waves at her.

When Sophia laughs, coos, or cries, she gains the immediate attention of a household of worshipers who rock her, pamper her, and provide child-care. Even as an infant, she senses that she is an important child of God. Born and raised in an intergenerational environment of the Christian house church, Sophia is blessed to be a part of a community where she is nurtured by several generations of believers.

One-year-old Alyssa was born into a Christian family in the city of Goodlettsville, Tennessee. Her family worships at Connell Memorial United Methodist Church where she was recently baptized. While at church, her parents James and Kelly need not worry about Alyssa getting all the attention she needs! Both maternal and paternal grandparents attend the church, along with her aunts and her uncle. Family members make sure Alyssa is well cared for. She smiles at her adopted grandmother and reaches out for the secure arms of Granny Joy, her nursery caregiver. Her pastors smile and greet her with enthusiasm and other church members watch to be sure she is safe as she happily explores her church environment.

Alyssa loves her time in the church nursery and she has bonded with her regular caregiver Granny Joy. Others in her church family care for her on a rotating basis in the church nursery, including parents of nursery children, parents of older children, "empty nesters," retired persons, singles, and older youth. Church is a happy place for Alyssa. Even as an infant she senses that she is an important child of God. Born and raised in an intergenerational environment of family and church, Alyssa is blessed to be a part of a faith community where she is nurtured by several generations.

Aaron, Sophia, and Alyssa are separated by time and place, but they have one thing in common. They are infants who are loved and cared for by many generations in their faith communities, including their own family members. However, most of the nursery age children who come to our churches today will not have the experiences of Aaron, Sophia, and Alyssa. They may have grandparents who live long distances from them. Their relatives may be scattered in several congregations or may not attend church at all. Some of our nursery children come from divorced families and may spend time in our church nursery as well as another church nursery. They may have little contact with persons of different generations unless we provide it for them in the church nursery and the congregation.

Relationships are important in the body of Christ. We are bound to one another as brothers and sisters in Christ because of God's love for us. What better way to model this for your congregation than to begin in the church nursery? What does your church nursery look like? Are the volunteers only women or do you have some men? Did you recruit only parents of nursery children as volunteers or are you using a wide-range of generations as nursery volunteers? Allow your nursery children to have the benefit of being blessed by the care and contact with many generations in your congregation. By doing so, you demonstrate to the entire church that intergenerational sharing is vital to the life of the congregation.

Recruiting Nursery Volunteers

Childcare experts tell us that children need certain key factors present in their lives to help them succeed. Children's advocates call these developmental assets. Developmental assets help children become competent, caring adults. Among them are family support, caring neighborhoods, and a child's emerging self-esteem that says, "I am a person of worth."

One of the assets that benefits infants and toddlers is especially important as we consider intergenerational nursery care in the church. Infants and toddlers must have positive adult relationships. Researchers inform us that infants and toddlers need love and nurture from at least one adult other than their parents. Furthermore, parents of nursery children need support. They do best in their parenting efforts when they aided by three or more adults. Our nurseries can provide infants, toddlers, and their parents with supportive adult relationships from several generations because most of the time persons from several generations are a part of our congregations.[1]

Many churches choose to use both paid and volunteer staff for their nursery. Infants and toddlers benefit from a familiar face that provides them with consistent care. The paid nursery workers can take away some of the anxiety or uncertainty that volunteers may feel when they serve in the nursery on what is usually a rotating basis. Besides the regular paid nursery workers or workers, who should you recruit as volunteers in your church nursery? Your goal should be to secure volunteers from several generations in your congregation and offer them training that will help them serve effectively in the church nursery. If you have not done so, it is time to expand your list of volunteers so your nursery children can have contact with several generations.

Parents as Nursery Workers

Parents of nursery children are usually willing to serve in the nursery because they feel that they need to volunteer their services in appreciation for the excellent care you are giving their child. Parents can often make good volunteers because they are experienced in providing childcare for an infant and toddler. They know how to change diapers and feed babies. Having parents of nursery children also allows them the opportunity to advocate for your nursery and express concerns when they have problems. They are able to observe firsthand what is going on in the nursery. Some churches request that anyone having a child in the nursery should be a part of the volunteer schedule.

Some parents would prefer not to work in the nursery for a variety of reasons. Some stay-at-home moms are tired and need time for rest and worship. Some parents are already committed in teaching or serving in Sunday school or worship. Try as best you can to be respectful of the desires of these parents even if your church policy suggests that they volunteer. You might try to schedule these parents a limited number of times or not at all. Sometimes reluctant parents will be more willing to serve as a nursery volunteer if they feel connected to the nursery ministry and when they believe that the nursery ministry is meeting the needs of their child. Give these parents something to do to keep them associated with your church nursery and they may be willing to volunteer at a later time.

If parents of nursery children are reluctant to volunteer in the church nursery, they can be recruited to clean toys or launder the crib sheets. They might also help with calling to recruit volunteers or scheduling volunteers. Some may want to serve on your nursery committee.

When you recruit parents, you might suggest to them that this is an excellent way to get to know other parents in the church and to get to know the church nursery staff. Newer parents can become more comfortable with babies and learn parenting skills when paired with more experienced parents. Obviously, this is an excellent way for parents to learn what is happening in the nursery and become familiar with nursery policies.

Some spouses would prefer to work together, and this offers an opportunity to involve more men in the nursery. Child abuse prevention policies often state that spouses are not to work alone together in a room with children. If this is the case with your policy, be sure that a paid worker or other volunteers are present when the spouses are scheduled for nursery duty together.

Parents of Older Children

Parents of children who are no longer a part of the nursery make excellent volunteers because they already have experience in childcare. They may not have children in the nursery area anymore, but enjoy having the contact with babies once again. When you recruit parents of children as volunteers, be sure they understand that they are not allowed to bring their older children with them into the nursery. This can disrupt the nursery environment and create safety concerns for infants and toddlers. If parents cannot abide by this rule, they should not be recruited to work in the nursery. The nursery environment is not the place for older children. Be sure that your church has activities for older children outside the nursery staffed by competent volunteers or paid workers. You will probably not have to worry about this during Sunday school. During worship time, provide a Children's Worship program for older children and do not forget to provide activities for older children during special events. Your parents of older children will be much more likely to serve as nursery volunteers when you provide activities for their older children.

Men as Nursery Volunteers

Using men in the church nursery will benefit both the babies and those who volunteer. Some babies respond better to men than to women. Young children will often come into contact with women as nurturers and teachers. The paid workers in most church nurseries are women. Women make up the majority of workers in daycare settings. Usually the teachers of young children will be women. Some of the nursery children may come from homes where there is not a father present. Infants and toddlers benefit from contact with Christian men who provide role models for them. Babies and toddlers need to know that both women and men love them and can be trusted to care for them.

Men who volunteer in the church nursery have the opportunity to learn better how to play, listen, watch, and interact with young children.

Some men may resist the idea of serving in the nursery. They may feel anxiety and worry that they are unable to provide the care that children need. You can assure these men that they will be working with a trained, competent nursery worker and other volunteers. Fathers whose children are in the nursery can be asked to serve as well as can men of all ages. Men whose children are grown often make excellent nursery workers, as do retired men who are grandfathers. Given that many nursery children may have grandparents who live distances from them, these "empty-nesters" and grandfathers give children contact with persons who remind them of their grandparents. They often give children unrushed care and unconditional love.

Some churches may be reluctant to use men to work with young children, perhaps thinking that parents will feel more comfortable with women caregivers. Churches may also be fearful of possible abuse allegations. Scheduling men with their spouse or with other women caregivers should alleviate this concern. Remind your congregation that Jesus provided a powerful image of a man being involved with little ones as he blessed the children. The men in your congregation can be advocates for the nursery when they are involved as volunteers and observe firsthand the excellent care the children are receiving. As other men in your church observe these respected men volunteering in the nursery, they, too, will be much more likely to become volunteers.

What About Youth Volunteers?

Your church may have a policy that no one under the age of eighteen may work or volunteer in the church nursery. If this is the case, work closely with your nursery coordinator and paid nursery worker to enforce this policy. There will be times when adult volunteers wish to bring their teenage children with them to help. If your church does not allow this, you must explain this to the adult volunteer. Having a policy in writing that you have shared with volunteers may alleviate this problem.

If you do allow youth to serve as volunteers you will want to be clear in writing at what age youth may serve in the nursery. Some teenagers will surprise you with what they know about caring for children. They may have younger siblings or have extensive baby-sitting experience. It is still a good idea to have a training session for all teen volunteers. Holding a special training session for the teenager volunteers held separate from the training for adult volunteers is helpful. Teenagers bring unique gifts and have special concerns that can be addressed in their own training session.

One of the advantages of having teens in the nursery is that being younger than your adult volunteers, they are often more willing to get down on the floor and spend time playing with the children. Yet they also must be made to realize that working in the nursery is a privilege and a responsibility.

During your training session with youth, communicate to them that nursery duty is not the time to socialize with other youth. They are in the nursery to care for the children. It is not a good idea to schedule several youth at the same time for nursery work. Put youth with a mature adult who can help them. This also gives youth the opportunity to come to know some adults in the church that will become new friends. You will want to go over the nursery policies with the youth. Some churches offer a child-care course for youth which provides them additional helpful training they can use when they babysit in the community.

Youth leaders and your youth director can guide you in selecting youth volunteers. The person scheduling the youth should make sure that they are not put on the rotation schedule so often that they frequently miss worship or Sunday school. Parents are often not pleased when they find that their youth does not attend church or Sunday school on a regular basis because he or she is scheduled for nursery duty. Be sure parents approve before you put any youth on the nursery schedule and check with parents to find out how often they wish for their youth to work in the nursery.

GUIDELINES FOR TEENAGE NURSERY VOLUNTEERS:

- Establish what age teenagers must be to work in the nursery.
- Consult with your youth director to recommend youth to work in the nursery.
- Do not schedule youth to work often. They need to be in Sunday school and worship.
- Put teenagers with adult workers not with other teens.
- Start out teenagers in the nursery by having them work first with toddlers, especially if they have little experience working with children.
- Seek approval of parents before teenagers are allowed to work in the nursery.
- Do not allow teenagers to bring any friends into the nursery even if these are visitors to the church.
- Do not allow teenagers to bring his/her girlfriend/boyfriend with them to help in the nursery.

- Do not allow teenagers to bring snacks into the nursery. (This applies to adult workers as well.)
- No cell phones allowed in the nursery. (This applies to adult workers as well.) Provide an emergency phone in the nursery area or allow the paid nursery workers to have a phone for emergency use only.
- Do not allow teenagers to chew gum in the nursery. (This applies to adult workers as well.)
- Ask youth to wear proper attire for the nursery. No skimpy clothes. Shoes must be worn at all times.
- Ask youth to remove all earrings or jewelry that would hurt children. (This applies to adult workers as well.)
- If you have a curriculum for toddlers and older youth, allow teenage volunteers to have experience teaching part of the curriculum.
- Provide a training event for youth volunteers. Have nursery rules for youth in writing.

Other Nursery Volunteers

Do not forget to recruit volunteers from all areas of your church life. Look for "empty-nesters" whose children are already grown, but enjoy working with young children. They do not have to worry about getting children ready for church on Sunday and can arrive at the nursery relaxed and ready to help. Ask some singles to help in the nursery. Even if they do not have children of their own, they often have baby-sitting experience or have cared for siblings. Grandmothers and grandfathers are sometimes overlooked when it comes to nursery volunteers, but they can be excellent at rocking babies or telling Bible stories to toddlers. Some older adults may have some physical constraints that would prevent them from lifting children. They can still volunteer in the nursery as long as they are paired with a worker who can help them.

Recruiting Across Generations

Once your church has decided that the nursery should be intergenerational you must recruit volunteers with that intention. For safety reasons, it is best to use volunteers who have regularly attended your church for a minimum of six months to a year. If someone unknown to you requests to help in the nursery explain the church policy. You can also suggest that this person help in others ways in your nursery until this person meets the time criteria for being considered as a nursery volunteer.

You can recruit by visiting the Sunday school classes and groups within the church and passing around a sign-up paper. Be aware, though, that you take a risk when you ask persons to sign up. You will more than likely find persons on the list that you do not think have the skills or temperament to work in the nursery. You can also advertise your need in the church newsletter or bulletin, but again, you may hurt a person's feelings when they volunteer to help and you do not think they are the right choice for working in the nursery. Churches can alleviate this problem by screening volunteer nursery workers. Ask volunteers to fill out a volunteer application form. The form asks the volunteer to describe his or her experience with children, state how long they have attended the church, and to answer questions about why they desire to volunteer in the nursery. The form can also ask for a statement of faith and references if desired. Always ask if the person has ever been convicted of a crime. You do not want anyone working with children who have a background of criminal or sexual abuse.

Churches can request a background check on all volunteers in the church nursery. This background check is a must for paid workers. Liability issues today have led many churches to require a background check on volunteer and paid workers. Your nursery committee must decide if you want to make this a mandatory requirement for working in the nursery. If you follow this procedure you must be consistent, even if you know a volunteer very well. Some persons who have been members of your church for several years may be insulted that you require a background check for them. You must explain that the reason for the background check is for the safety of the children and is not meant to imply that the church does not trust their character.

While a sign-up sheet or advertisement can give you many persons across generations, selecting persons who have been suggested by church leaders is often the best way to find your nursery workers. After recommendations have been made, you can ask these persons if they would agree to serve by calling them on the phone, by emailing them, or by asking them in person. Be sure and explain the requirements and policies of your nursery area. If your church requires it, you will still need to ask these persons to complete a volunteer application and secure a background check on them.

When a background check is conducted on a volunteer or paid worker, keep documentation of this information in a confidential place in the church. Your police department or sheriff's department can help you with reports of abuse, or they can direct your church to the agency in your community that does background checks. There is usually a fee associated with these background checks, so your church will need to budget for this.

Whatever method you use to recruit volunteers and whatever your requirements, screening volunteer nursery workers with the same standards you use to screen paid workers will go a long way in assuring that problems with volunteers is kept to a minimum. This careful process also gives parents the confidence that they can leave their children in the nursery without worry. This also communicates to them and the entire congregation that you place a high value on the nursery child.

Scheduling Across Generations

Selecting and recruiting an intergenerational group of nursery volunteers allows you to schedule persons from different generations to work together. When you make up your volunteer schedule, think carefully about the persons who will work together. Pair inexperienced parents with experienced parents or grandparents. Have a teenager work with a grandparent so he or she can become friends with an older adult in the church. Have a parent who needs babysitting services work with a teenager who might be a good babysitter for the family. Have "empty-nesters" work with singles. Mix up the generations so they can encourage each other and enjoy serving together. Your caregivers will be more likely to continue to serve in the nursery when they have had positive experiences.

Take into account the physical constraints and time restrictions of your nursery volunteers. You may have a grandparent who has limited physical strength that could work with a healthy youth or adult. Think about the commitments your nursery volunteers have made in other areas of your congregation. Some of your volunteers serve in many ways in your congregation. They might serve on several committees, teach Sunday school, or lead in children's worship. Be sure you do not schedule them as often as others whose primary area of service is the church nursery. Develop a schedule for six to twelve months at a time. Send this schedule to the volunteers, but also send a weekly reminder by postcard, email, or a phone call.

Be certain that you schedule adequate workers for the number of children in the nursery rooms. Any nursery room, no matter how small, should be staffed by at least two adults. Three adults in each nursery room allows for one adult who is available to leave the room if needed. Child abuse prevention policies recommend two adults with children at all times and if spouses are working together, one other additional adult. Experts recommend the following child/worker ratio:

Infants (0-6months):	Two babies/One adult worker
Crawlers (6-12 months):	Three babies/One adult worker
Toddlers (12-18 months):	Four toddlers/One adult worker
Walkers (18-24 months):	Five or six children/One adult worker
Three-Four Year Old:	Six to nine children/One adult worker[3]

Child Abuse Prevention Policy

Every church should develop a policy concerned with the safety of children. Churches may call this a *Safe Sanctuary Policy* or *Child Abuse Prevention Policy*. Whatever the name, your policy should educate the congregation about the different forms of child abuse, give them signs to look for that might signal potential child abuse, and provide them ways to prevent child abuse. This policy should be in writing and shared with all volunteers you recruit for the church nursery.

If your church has never developed such a policy, form a committee made up of key leaders in the church. You should include a member of the Trustees and either your nursery coordinator or the chair of your children's ministry team. Some churches find it helpful to have health professionals on the committee. Some churches request that a lawyer knowledgeable in liability issues review the policy and the safety measures the church has developed. If your nursery is licensed by your state to serve children in daycare, you will always want to follow state health and safety regulations whenever your nursery is in use for daycare purposes.

Once you have selected your committee you will need to find resources to help you develop your policy. Many denominations now have their own policies, which can be taken and adapted for the local church. Check with your denominational office to see if such a policy exists. There may also be a person who is trained and willing to come to your church and provide you with information on what needs to be included in your abuse prevention policy. An excellent resource is *Safe Sanctuaries, Reducing the Risk of Child Abuse in the Church* written by Joy Thornburg Melton (Discipleship Resources). This book contains a biblical and theological mandate for the safety of all children. Provided is a plan on how your committee can develop policies/procedure and forms for screening workers, checking references, and reporting suspected child abuse. This resource also contains suggestions for ways to train workers with children and a sample worship service that can be used when you adopt the policy.

As you recruit several generations to work in the church nursery, they must all be trained in the child abuse prevention policy. This must be a requirement for volunteering in the nursery. Inform all volunteers of the "two adult rule." This rule states that no fewer than two adults can be present in the church nursery at all times. For additional safety, require that the two adults not be related. If they are, secure another adult to work with these volunteers. Keeping this rule in mind will help in scheduling different generations of volunteers. Youth will need to be present with two adults who are not related to one another. Other important safety measures to consider would be:

- Provide first-aid and CPR training at least once a year for all nursery volunteers.
- Train workers at least annually in all nursery policies. Provide a separate training for youth nursery volunteers.
- Some churches stipulate that no nursery volunteers can be under the age of eighteen. You will have to make this decision as to whether you will use youth volunteers or not.
- Place windows in nursery doors or a half door.
- Window blinds should be open and doors should remain unlocked.
- Have nursery volunteers wear a name badge.[4]

One issue that sometimes arises is whether a person who has been found guilty of child molestation in the past, but has radically changed, can ever be used as a volunteer in the church nursery. Putting this person in the nursery is taking an enormous risk, no matter how much time has passed since the offense. There are places in the church where this individual can serve effectively; the church nursery is not one of these places.

As we work to provide a safe environment for our nursery children our rules and regulations seem to indicate that we prefer a "hands-off" approach when it comes to the children. It is impossible to work in the nursery and not touch children as they are carried, rocked, and diapered. Your volunteers need to be instructed in the ways they are allowed to touch children and what is considered inappropriate. Here are some of the guidelines you can share with them.

APPROPRIATE WAYS TO TOUCH IN THE NURSERY

- Bend down to the child's eye level and talk kindly to the child. Listen to toddlers and older nursery children as they share with you.
- Take the hand of a child and lead him or her to an activity.
- Rock babies to sleep or to soothe them when crying or upset.

- Carry babies around the room gently.
- Change diapers gently, cleaning the child using wipes. Always wear gloves when changing diapers and wash your hands afterward.
- Put your arm around the shoulders of a toddler or older nursery child who is upset or needs to be comforted.
- Hold a toddler or nursery child who is crying.
- Help a child who is potty trained if he/she needs help with clean-up or washing hands. Keep the door ajar for safety purposes, so other volunteers in the nursery might be aware of your actions, but not wide enough that it would embarrass the child in any way.

INAPPROPRIATE TOUCH TO BE AVOIDED IN THE NURSERY:

- Never kiss a child, coax a child to kiss you, or give a child an extended hug.
- Never tickle children.
- Never touch a nursery child in any area that would be covered by a bathing suit with the exception of the times when you are helping a potty trained child with toileting.
- Be sure you are never alone in the room with a nursery child.[5]

Persons who are hesitant to volunteer in the church nursery will be much more willing to do so when you provide them training and have safety measures in place. These safety measures are for the protection of the children as well as the volunteers.

Intergenerational Sharing for Congregations

Generations working together in the church nursery must be extended to generations working together in your church. Reaching across generations in the nursery must expand to all areas of church life. Following the example of intergenerational sharing in the nursery, your church should strive to create a family atmosphere where all are welcomed and included.

Worship

Although several generations may meet together for worship, this does not mean we are necessarily interacting with one another. Churches should encourage older adults to help families with their children during worship. A caring adult or a friendly youth can be a good helper for parents during worship. If you have a children's message in your service, recruit volunteers from several age groups in your church to share. However, be sure these persons are trained. Only use persons who understand how to communicate with children in a worship setting. If you have a Children's Worship time in which the children go out of the sanctuary, use volunteers from different generations. Pair older adults with the parents of children so they can work together in Children's Worship. Ask mature youth to serve occasionally. Be sure you ask men to serve as volunteers also.

Sunday School

Encourage several generations in the church to be involved in teaching children and youth in Sunday school. Older youth and college students are good role models and children enjoy their presence in the classroom. Grandparents can be recruited as helpers in the classrooms or to share faith stories and experiences with the children.

Some churches offer intergenerational classes where children and parents meet together for lessons. If your denomination does not provide curriculum to use when different generations meet together, you might consider using *Sunday School Special* (4 volumes) by Lois Keffer (Group Publishing).

Encourage adult Sunday school classes to adopt children and youth classes in the church. Have the class host a fellowship-get acquainted time with the children and youth. Members of the adult class could substitute for the regular teacher from time to time to give him or her a break. They could also purchase items for the class that are not a part of the Sunday school budget.

Adopt-A-Grandparent Program

An Adopt-a-Grandparent program in your church is an excellent way to bring generations together for fellowship, support, and learning. Children and youth adopt senior adults in the church. Your church can plan activities throughout the year in which the adopted grandchildren, adopted grandparents, and family members can share together. You can find detailed information on how to set up an adopted grandparent program, forms to use for signing up participants, and answers to the questions/concerns that may arise in the book *The Children's Minister* (Discipleship Resources) written by this author.

Fellowship Events

Plan several fellowship events throughout the year that are church-wide and involve several generations. This could be a birthday party where persons are asked to sit at the decorated table for the month they were born. There are a myriad of other activities you can plan to bring generations together such as picnics, ice cream socials, movie night, music events, square dancing, and game night.

Wednesday Night Dinners & Activities

Wednesday night dinners provide the opportunity for generations to gather for a meal. Be sure to encourage families to sit with older adults or persons they do not know in the church. Plan some activities immediately after dinner before persons leave the table. Encourage adults to help families of children with getting their dinners and carrying them to the table. A parent who is carrying an infant appreciates the help of a youth or adults in getting food for other children in the family or helping the parent get his or her dinner. Adults in the church family might hold infants so the parents can enjoy their meal. If your church does not have Wednesday night dinners, you can plan potlucks after church to provide opportunities for generations in your church to fellowship together.

Work Day

Plan a work day periodically, in which all ages in your congregation are invited to participate. Encourage children and youth to be present. Children can work alongside adults who will supervise them and teach them important labor skills. Children and youth appreciate adults who are patient and who will praise them for their efforts. They are proud to have a part in making their church a more appealing place, and they are especially pleased to be included in events that are important to the congregation as a whole.

Mission Outreach Projects

Most children and youth in your congregation will enjoy working with adults of all ages in mission outreach projects. Older adults can organize a mission outreach project and invite children to work with them. The women of the church should invite girls to be a part of their mission efforts and the men of the church should encourage boys to participate in their outreach endeavors. If your church has a tape ministry where homebound members receive a video of your worship service, recruit families in the church to deliver these tapes. In this way the children in the family can have contact with a homebound member.

Intergenerational Learning Events

The seasons of the church year lend themselves very well to intergenerational learning events. During the season of Advent, plan a church-wide event, bringing all generations in the church together. Persons can put together an Advent wreath, make symbols for the season, and learn together about the meaning of Advent. Have persons come to the church during Epiphany for an Epiphany Fair. During this event, persons of all ages can participate in activities that help them learn about the wise men. On Shrove Tuesday, serve pancakes, share about the meaning of Lent, and provide activities that persons can do together during Lent to serve others. Suggest to the senior adults in the church that they host an Easter egg hunt for the children. Involve the youth in stuffing eggs, hiding them, and playing games with the children. Involve as many age groups in the church as possible. Celebrate Pentecost with a church-wide party for all generations in the church.

Church-wide Retreat

An annual church-wide retreat can bring together generations in the church. Held in the relaxed setting of a camp, this event affords persons the opportunity to get to know one another in the congregation outside of the church setting. If you want senior adults to attend, you need to consider housing and handicap-accessible facilities. Many senior adults will not attend a retreat if the rooms are not comfortable and equipped with bathroom facilities. Many camps now have "motel-like" rooms with bathrooms inside the rooms. Plan activities where all ages can interact with one another.

Vacation Bible School

Vacation Bible school can become an intergenerational event. Encourage your director to be certain to recruit volunteers from several age groups within the church. Another way to make the event intergenerational is to provide activities for adults at the same time the children are in Vacation Bible school. Even though not all of your adults will be working with the children, having adults of all ages present at Vacation Bible School creates a family-like atmosphere. Serve a family style meal each night if your Vacation Bible School takes place in the evening.

Men and Women's Groups

Men and women's groups in your church can plan special events that include children and youth. Men might organize father-son banquet and women a mother-daughter banquet. Be sensitive in your planning to children who have lost a parent. Have a woman or man reach out to these children and invite them to attend the event. If you do not want to call it a father-son or mother-daughter banquet, then just have a special event for all generations in the church of the same gender. This can become an annual event that men and women of all generations look forward to in your church.

Other Suggestions

- Cooking classes held together for children, youth, and adults.
- Craft classes held together for children, youth, and adults.
- Christmas caroling where all ages carol together.
- Sewing or knitting classes led by adults for children and youth.
- Blessing of the Animals service where all ages are encouraged to participate. (Pets are brought to the church and blessed by the pastors in a brief service. Detailed information on the Blessings of the Animals service may be found in the book *The Children's Minister* (Discipleship Resources)
- Woodworking or pottery classes held together for children, youth, and adults.
- Decorating the sanctuary together for special seasons such as Advent or Easter.
- Place children, youth, and adults together on a committee to prepare the Communion elements for worship.
- Place children, youth, and adults together on a committee to prepare the altar for worship during special seasons and events of the church year.
- Use different generations to serve as ushers and greeters in the worship service.

- Have an intergenerational choral ensemble or hand-bell choir to perform in worship on occasion.
- If you have a prayer garden at your church, ask children, youth, and adults to work together to weed the garden and plant flowers.

Relationships in the Church and Nursery

All generations have a place in the life of the church. All generations need one another. We are blessed by the presence of other fellow believer who may be different from us, but who bring insights and experiences that enrich us. All of us need the wisdom and friendship of different ages in the church. Nursery children grow and develop in faith when they have generations of people who care for them. When emulated by the entire congregation, this pattern of intergenerational caring and sharing can form your people into the body of Christ. At church we may call ourselves the "family of God", but our actions may prove otherwise. What better way to practice family in the church than by finding ways for generations to interact with one another?

Family life is never perfect; it can be messy, problematic, and, at times, risky. Are we willing to risk in the life of our church to bring generations together? What we will discover is that along with the risk comes relationships that might never have developed had we not made room in our church life for generations to be together in ministry.

Paul constantly reminds us in his writings of the relationships that should exist between the followers of Christ. Paul uses the words "one another" over and over again to remind us of the importance of relationships. We are to love one another, pray for one another, accept one another, comfort one another, care for one another, teach one another, be kind to one another, and forgive one another. The fellowship of believers described in Acts 2:42-47 provide an amazing picture of a community of faith that truly cares for one another as brothers and sisters in Christ. This passage speaks of all believers, all generations, coming together for worship, teaching, fellowships, meals, and prayer. They enjoyed being with one another. They gathered in each other's home, ate together, and were concerned about each other's needs. This can happen in our churches when we provide opportunities for intergenerational sharing and when we allow the spirit of God to move among the generations in our church, bringing us together in harmonious relationships of love and respect.

Chapter Six Endnotes

1. Jolene L. Roehlkepartain & Nancy Leffert. *What Young Children Need to Succeed: Working Together to Build Assets from Birth to Age 11* (Minneapolis: Free Spirit Publishing, Inc., 2000), 38.
2. Jennifer Root Wilger, *The Safe and Caring Church Nursery* (Loveland: Group Publishing Co., 1998), 75.
3. Laura J. Brown, "Protecting Kids is a Priority: Church Nursery Security Makes the Best Possible First Impression on Parents." 31 May 2007, 2 Sept. 2008 [http://www.churchsolutionsmag.com/article/risk-management/75h3116552876338.html].
4. Melton, Joy Thornburg. *Safe Sanctuaries: Reducing the Risk of Child Abuse in the Church* (Nashville: Discipleship Resources, 1989), 32-33.
5. Scottie May, Beth Posterski, Catherine Stonehouse & Linda Cannell. *Children Matter: Celebrating Their Place in the Church, Family, and Community* (Grand Rapids, Wm. B. Eerdmans Publishing Co., 2005), 322.

Chapter Seven

PRACTICE WHAT YOU PREACH

Taking Seriously Vows of Infant Baptism

Sixth grader David has faithfully participated for several months in his church's confirmation class in preparation for the time in which he will profess his faith and claim for himself the vows of church membership. His pastors, Rev. Neal and Rev. Rita have shared with him and his classmates about the beliefs and history of their denomination, along with an understanding of the sacraments of the church. The time is quickly approaching when the confirmation class will stand before the church, saying "yes" to the vows that their parents and church family said on their behalf when they were baptized as infants.

Their pastors have told them that when they say their vows on Pentecost Sunday they are to stand facing the congregation. They are to look out at the faces of their friends, their Sunday school teachers, their Vacation Bible school leaders, their parents, and their mentors in the faith. Why? Pastor Neal and Rev. Rita want David and the rest of the class to recognize that the very people facing them are the same ones who took vows to nurture, support, and raise them in the Christian faith before they were even aware of this promise.

David likes this idea. Baptized as an infant and raised in the life of his congregation, he has always been an active part of this community of faith. His positive experiences of church began in the nursery, continued into childhood, and are now strengthened as he approaches youth age. David understands that he would never have been where he is today in his faith journey had not so many people in his congregation made good on the vows they said at his baptism.

Time and again his pastors have used two words in the confirmation class to describe baptism: gift and grace. Marked as a child of God through the waters of his baptism, David will live his life and enter his death marked with the gift of grace. Baptism and grace are powerful gifts that remind David that he belongs to God.

When David was born, his parents arrived at the nursery door, placing David in the arms of trusted caregivers who would partner with them to guide David in his faith journey. Today, Christian parents will arrive at your nursery door, placing their baptized infants in your arms and expecting you to uphold the vows taken at the baptism of these children. Will you do this? A clear understanding of infant baptism and the vows you have taken will help nursery caregivers fulfill the promises made by the congregation at the baptism of infants.

Understanding Infant Baptism

Infant baptism stems from our understanding of God's grace; an unmerited gift of God. In baptism, God reaches out to our infants and claims them as God's own children. God knows them by name and begins the work of grace in their lives. God initiates this gift in the life of each child. God is the chief actor and agent in baptism, not the ministers, the parents, or the congregation, even if all of these persons have vital roles to play. In baptism we sees God's actions toward the child: reaching, claiming, naming, calling, and nurturing. God is extending grace to each child in his or her baptism.

God's grace is evident in the life of each child, through what John Wesley, the founder of the Methodist movement, called prevenient grace. Wesley taught that through prevenient grace God reaches out to each child before he or she was even aware of this grace at work. In infant baptism, God's prevenient grace is evident as is each infant is marked as a child of God and begins the journey of faith.

Infant baptism reminds us that we are dependent upon divine grace. God takes the initiative to reach out to us and bring us into relationship with our Maker. Infants are incapable of responding to God's grace, yet God reaches out in spite of the infant's inability to respond to God. Infants are totally dependent on God's gift of grace, demonstrating to all of us our dependence on God for our salvation.

In baptism, infants enter into a new life in Christ as children of God and members of the body of Christ. Baptism incorporates an infant into the community of faith. Baptism is an early step in that infant's lifelong journey of faith.

The Parent's Role in Infant Baptism

Infants are baptized in the Wesleyan tradition only when they come from homes where the parents or guardians are Christians and will take responsibility for raising their children in the Christian faith. John Wesley wrote a great deal about the nurture of children in the home, admonishing parents to take this role seriously. He also urged all parents to take infant baptism seriously and to bring their children to the church to be baptized at an early age.

Your pastor will not only administer the sacrament of infant baptism, but also will be an advocate for infant baptism for all young children. The nursery caregiver and nursery coordinator can keep the pastor informed of new families in the nursery whose children may not have received the sacrament of baptism.

In the United Methodist tradition, when infants are brought to the congregation and presented for baptism, the parents are asked several important questions. The first question asks parents to declare their own faith in Jesus Christ as their personal Savior. Parents cannot be spiritual guides unless they themselves have a strong commitment to Christ. The second question asked of parents affirms the necessity of parents taking seriously their role as spiritual educators. Parents are asked to be role models for their children by setting an example of how to live the Christian life. They commit themselves to raising the child in the Christian faith, teaching them the words of Scripture, and not only bringing the children to worship, but also regularly attending themselves. Parents agree to have private worship in their homes as well as attending worship with fellow believers in the body of Christ.

The questions asked of parents at the baptism of their children are not to be taken lightly. The promises to raise children in the Christian faith, teach them the Scripture, and to bring them to worship all involve time and effort. The most demanding question asked of parents, however, is whether they will live before the child a life that becomes the gospel. That is the real work of spiritual guidance. The faith of the parents is what provides the nurture for the faith of the child.

If a parent or sponsor cannot and will not nurture the child in the faith, then baptism is to be postponed until Christian nurture is available. A child who dies without being baptized is received into the love and presence of God because the Spirit has worked in that child to bestow grace. If a child has been baptized, but his family or sponsors do not faithfully nurture the child in the faith, then the congregation, especially through its nursery, has a responsibility for incorporating the child into its life and teaching the child the ways of God.

The Role of the Congregation in Infant Baptism

When we baptize infants, our congregation should be places that are ready to receive these little ones into the life of the church. The congregation makes a lifelong commitment to the parent and children, vowing to be involved in the life of each child. The congregation agrees to help families with spiritual development and to support them in their efforts to raise their children in the Christian faith.

In the United Methodist tradition, the parents are not the only ones who take a vow in infant baptism; the congregation takes an extremely important vow as well. The pastor asks the congregation if they will nurture one another in the faith, but also include the infant being baptized in their care. The congregation promises to provide the infant with a community of love and forgiveness and to set an example of Christ-like living. Furthermore, they promise to pray for the child so that the infant, nurtured in the church and surrounded by a supportive community of faith, will one day decide for himself or herself to follow Christ.

The congregation adopts the child as their own. No longer does the child belong just to the family, but also to an entire congregation which promises to support each child in his or her nurture and to partner with parents in providing faith formation for each child.

From our understanding of infant baptism and the role of the congregation in the life of each child, we reach out to each child and to his or her parents. We view each child as our own and, along with the parents, seek to guide the child in the Christian faith. We invest in the life of each child. We covenant to become partners with the parents. We recognize that the way we nurture, teach, and care for each child can influence the child in his or her future decision to follow Christ.

Nursery workers should be committed to pray for each child, just as the congregation has vowed. They should also realize that they are role models for the child in Christ-like living as is the congregation. Caregivers in the nursery must extend forgiveness and love to each child following the example of the congregation's vow at a child's baptism.

Your training time for nursery workers should include a session on infant baptism. Nursery workers are included in the congregational vows as much as any member of the congregation. Nursery workers, like the congregation, have ongoing responsibilities for the child and the child's family. Just as Christ receives us, we receive each child who comes to our nursery. Just as a congregation of faith rejoices when a child is baptized, we celebrate in the nursery. We take seriously our vows to raise this child in the Christian faith just as the congregation as a whole and the parents promise. Understanding the baptismal vows reinforces to nursery caregivers how vital their role is in the lives of the nursery children.

Not every child that arrives at our nursery doors and not every child that we care for in the nursery will have been baptized as infants. However, we should extend the promises we make to baptized children to any child in the nursery. Each child is under the grace of God whether he or she has been baptized as an infant.

John Wesley believed that baptism is not a requirement for salvation. Our salvation is a free gift of God that comes through Christ. God can and does work both through and outside of the sacraments, both through and outside of the church. However, this does not mean that baptism is unimportant or optional. God has chosen to give us the gift of baptism and we should rejoice when a child is baptized, yet continue to extend grace to each child regardless of whether or not he or she is baptized as an infant.

Confirmation and Re-baptism

One aspect of the upcoming confirmation service is bothering David, the young man mentioned at the beginning of this chapter. His pastors have told the class that since all of the confirmands were baptized as infants, they will renew their baptism by touching water. Rev. Rita will say, "Remember your baptism and be thankful." The only problem for David is that he does not remember his baptism. He strongly believes he must be re-baptized.

Often persons in your church, like David, will struggle with the issue of re-baptism. They wrestle with the answers to questions about their own baptism. Since they cannot remember their baptism, they wonder if their baptism was as significant an event as it was for the person who was baptized as a youth or adult. After all, persons baptized as youth and adults had a say in their baptisms. Surely an event as important as baptism needs to be remembered, does it not? Can this sacrament hold meaning for those who were baptized as infants, given that these individuals did nothing on their part except show up with their parents and family? These questions are real issues for some of the believers in our churches. We must never take their struggles lightly.

David's pastors shared with him and the confirmation class that in our United Methodist tradition we do not re-baptize. They went on to explain the reasons. God is the primary agent in our baptism. God acts in such a powerful way in our baptism even if we are not aware of God's actions. Infant baptism demonstrates God's grace extended to us when we can do absolutely nothing! Infants cannot respond to God in their baptism, yet God still reaches out in love and begins the work of grace in the life of each child. If we believe that God's actions toward us are good, then surely God got it just right in our baptism! For us to be re-baptized conveys the message that God did not fulfill God's part of the covenant so God somehow needs our actions as well.

Certainly God desires for each individual to respond in faith to God's saving acts in Jesus Christ. David will faithfully respond to God at his confirmation and will continue to respond to God throughout his life. Yet his baptism is a powerful reminder of God's covenant love expressed toward David. Remembering is not a prerequisite for receiving God's gifts of love and grace. If this were the case, we could never baptize an individual who faced mental challenges. David's inability to recall the details of his baptism does not make God's actions any less powerful. Someone with Parkinson or dementia cannot remember their baptism even if they were adults at the time. So, when his pastor says, "David, remember your baptism and be thankful," what can David remember that will make both his baptism and his confirmation meaningful for him?

David can remember his identity. Who is he? David is a chosen child of God. David has always been a child of God, but through his baptism he has been given a visible reminder. In some services of infant baptism the pastor will ask the family members, "What is the name of this child?" A pastor does not do this because he or she cannot remember the name of the child, but by calling the name of the child aloud, he or she reminds the parents and congregation that this child belongs to God. The baptized infant is identified as a child of God.

David can remember that he belongs. Through his baptism he has been incorporated into the body of Christ. He has inherited a history. All of those who came before David and all who will come after David are a part of his heritage in the church universal. In his baptism David's family grew much larger. All of his church family have taken on the responsibility of caring and nurturing David in his Christian faith, guiding him to this time in his life in which he will now affirm the good work of God in his life.

Confirmands should always be assigned a mentor during the confirmation journey. This person can guide and support the confirmand and his or her family. David's mentor was one of his Sunday school teachers, who vowed, when David was baptized, that he would support David and his family. This mentor faithfully carried out his responsibilities promised at David's baptism. His mentor continues to uphold the pledge he made to David and promises to do so in the future. He will stand with David when he is confirmed as a reminder of the fulfillment of congregational vows made to David at his infant baptism. His role does not stop with David's confirmation, however. His mentor will continue to offer support to David's family and to remain involved in David's life.

After David was baptized, his pastor carried him down the aisles of the sanctuary introducing David to his church family. As he did so, the pastor said, "David, here is your church family. When you need a Sunday school teacher, a Vacation Bible school leader, or a confirmation mentor, these people will be present for you." What a powerful way to remind the congregation of ways they are to carry out the vows of infant baptism! The promises made at the baptism of infants are more than words; they require action. David was blessed to be a part of a congregation that put words into action. David can remember that his congregation took seriously the vows made at his baptism.

David's parents shared with him about his baptism. They showed him pictures of the day he was baptized. In one picture, David notices that he wears the same gown worn by his grandfather and his father at their baptisms. He views photos of family members and church friends who gathered that day for his baptismal service and for the luncheon afterward. His family relates to him stories of that special day. His baby book contains his baptismal certificate signed by his pastors. All these visible reminders and stories help David remember his baptism and help him to be thankful.

In the same way, parents in your congregation should be encouraged to help their children remember their baptism. Remind them to show children pictures of their baptism and keep their baptismal certificates in a special place. Families can celebrate the anniversary of a child's baptism. Your church could video the service for the family. Some churches present a gift to the family such as a baptismal candle or shell (symbol for baptism).

The church nursery should celebrate the baptism of infants along with the congregation. Pictures of the baptism of your nursery infants can be displayed on a bulletin board outside your nursery door to be shared with the entire congregation. Arrange for the nursery caregiver that the child has bonded with to be present in the sanctuary for the baptism. Your nursery committee could send a card to the family when an infant is baptized. This chapter contains a list of suggestions for celebrating infant baptisms in your church family.

The Church and Home in Partnership

There is absolutely no way a congregation can fulfill the vows of infant baptism without showing support for parents. In infant baptism, we promise to help parents raise their child in the Christian faith. This promise begins in the church nursery when we provide the best environment for infants to grow in faith. Yet we can also partner with parents in the church and home. Churches can provide support classes, parenting classes, marriage classes, divorce recovery classes, and Bible study classes for parents. Childcare for any church event is a must. We can create an environment in worship where children and families are welcome. We continue to guide and nurture children throughout the preschool, elementary, and youth years, providing classes and activities to help them grow in their faith. Individuals of all generations should be selected to serve as role models for children and youth, interacting with them in the life of the church. All of these efforts are vital; yet, we must link the church with the home.

John Wesley strongly believed that the home was pivotal in the faith development of children. Wesley encouraged parents to take seriously the religious instruction of their children. He admonished both mothers and fathers to be involved in their children's faith formation. Wesley was certainly aware of the reality that religious education sometimes suffers in the home because of the limited ability or willingness of parents. Wesley encouraged the church to be involved in training and supporting parents in their vital role as religious educators. Wesley reminded his pastors that the care of infants is more important than preaching to an adult congregation. He required all of his preachers to establish family worship in every Methodist home. We must recover this Wesleyan understanding of the importance of supporting families as they seek to be spiritual educators of their children. Churches must do more than help parents when they are at church; they must provide resources for use in the home.[1]

The significant role of the home and family in the faith development of children is supported by the 1990 study by The Search Institute: *Effective Christian Education: A National Study of Protestant Congregations.* This study found that family faith was one of the most powerful indicators of growth in faith among adolescents and adults. Four hundred youth, ages 13 to 18, whose parents had established religious tradition in the home when these youth were children, were compared with four hundred youth whose parents had no active family faith. A marked contrast existed between those youth raised in homes where faith was expressed and those raised in homes where it was not practiced. Youth who were most likely to mature in their faith were those raised in homes where the faith was shared as a part of the normal activities and flow of family life.[2]

The study indicates that the nurturing quality of a home where faith is often expressed by the parents has a great deal of influence on children, and the impact is felt into the teenage and adult years. Religious practices in the home virtually doubles the probability of a congregation's youth entering into the life of a church and continuing to be loyal to the church when they reach adulthood. Faith shared in the home is not the only factor gathered from the youth responses in this study. Youth gave credit to the influence of their congregation as well.[3]

The Search Institute found congregational education to be extremely important for helping children, youth, and adults live out faith in family life. The study recognized the importance of family conversations about faith; thus, congregations should find ways to help families talk about their faith. The quality of worship and the quality of Christian education in the congregation were also factors that hindered or aided faith formation. Christian education in congregational life should help parents play a more active role in the religious education of their children. Congregations can help families become educated on how to use family conversations to talk about faith, in how to plan and carry out family devotionals, and how to take part in family service projects. They can also be given ideas on how to share in family activities while talking about faith.[4]

We recognize that our families live fast-paced lives. They rush from activity to activity, and their days are filled with hectic schedules. Families are often challenged to find time to sit down to eat a meal together, much less to find time to share about spiritual matters. Many parents perceive themselves as being unqualified to share faith matters with their children. Many do not know where to look for resources. Parents become overwhelmed when we admonish them to be spiritual educators of their children. For these reasons, and because we take seriously our commitment at the baptism of these children, we must help these families. In this chapter are some suggestions for churches to use as they partner with families in the home and a recommended list of helpful books.

Implications of Infant Baptism for the Entire Church

Understanding Our Salvation

Infant baptism teaches the church that our salvation is a gift from God. Whether we were baptized as infants or made the decision as youth and adults to follow Christ and be baptized, our salvation does not result from our own actions. Granted, our decision to follow Christ was the most important decision we made in our lives, so this decision should never be lessened. Yet we can get into the bind of speaking of our salvation experiences and our youth and adult baptisms as if we were responsible for them. Infants who are baptized cannot do anything to affect the saving waters of their baptism; they receive as a gift God's grace at work in their lives. Infant baptism causes us to examine our own baptism, at whatever point it occurred in our lives, and give thanks for the salvation of Christ freely offered to each of us. Remembering our baptism humbles us as we recognize that we are all children, claimed, and chosen by God, and created to serve God and others.

A Picture of Grace

Infant baptism gives us a picture of God's grace in the Wesleyan tradition. Infant baptism points to God's prevenient grace in the life of the church and the life of the child. God's prevenient grace, evident at the baptism of an infant, continues to work in the life of the child always. That is a reminder to us that God's prevenient grace works in our lives regardless of how and when we were baptized. Prevenient grace falls on us when we stray from God, bringing us back to a relationship with God. Prevenient grace, through the work of the Holy Spirit, convicts us of sin, offers us forgiveness, and helps us to extend grace to others. When a baptized infant, nurtured in the life of the church, makes the decision to follow Christ, God's justifying grace is at work. Yet, God's justifying grace is at work in all of our lives, regardless of our baptismal mode, to lead us to salvation in Christ and strengthen us in our growth as Christians. God's sanctifying grace leads us on toward the goal of Christian perfection, as we love God and one another.

All Are Responsible for Children in the Church

Each and every time a child is baptized in our congregations, we are reminded of our responsibility to care and mentor children in the Christian faith. Parents have primary responsibility, but all of us in the church must take seriously our role as nurturers. We set an example for children by the way we relate to one another in the church.

When we are asked to serve in some area in the children or youth's ministry, we must recognize that this is a serious commitment. We must think and pray about our decision. All of us have different gifts to share with the body of Christ. Some of us do not possess the gifts or temperament to work with children in certain areas. However, we must think very carefully before we exclude ourselves completely from contact with children in the church. Our lack of qualifications may prevent us from teaching Sunday school, but we might make a wonderful adopted grandparent for a child or youth. Perhaps we lack the skills or patience to serve in Children's Worship, but we can volunteer in the nursery. Our schedule may not allow us to serve as a confirmation mentor, but we can provide a meal for the youth. We must continually be examining the vows we took when infants were baptized. Are we keeping our promises or have we spoken empty words that have no meaning for us?

Events in the life of the church are a part of the baptismal work. Children, fully included in the life of the church, have their baptism confirmed every time they participate in the events of the church life. Potluck dinners, confirmation classes, worship, Adopt-a-Grandparent fellowship times, Holy Communion, sermons, Sunday school, Vacation Bible school and seasonal events; all of these and more point to the sacrament of baptism, as long as children are allowed to engage in them as active participants.[5]

Remembering Our Own Baptism

Since we do not re-baptize in our Wesleyan tradition, all of us are given the opportunity through our baptism to remember God's grace extended to us. We know in infant baptism that a child cannot remember his or her own baptism, yet we strongly affirm the need to remember our baptism as an act of thanksgiving. We may not remember certain elements of our baptism, such as what we wore and who was in attendance. Our family and church friends who were present can share these parts of our baptism with us. The essential part to remember is that we were offered the gift of God's grace and a community of faith surrounded us and never lets us forget we belong to God. We need one another as brothers and sisters in Christ. We need opportunities in the life of the church to remember our baptism.

Individuals can remember their baptism in corporate worship when we plan times throughout the year where persons can renew their baptismal covenant. The United Methodist Church has a *Renewal of Baptismal* service in The United Methodist Hymnal appropriate for the Baptism of our Lord Sunday, designated on the church calendar for the first Sunday after Epiphany. Yet on other occasions such as All Saints Day, Easter, or Pentecost, we can incorporate the renewal of baptismal vows into the worship service.

Baptism and Other Rituals of the Church

Holy Communion is also a sacrament of the church in which God's grace is evident. In the United Methodist Church we practice open communion. All persons regardless of age, background, or religious tradition are invited to our table. Since this meal of hospitality is also a family meal, and our church family consists of baptized persons, there is a clear link between baptism and Holy Communion. Communion remembers God's grace given to us in our baptism, but it also celebrates God's sustaining presence with us as we remember Christ's sacrifice for each of us. John Wesley believed that an individual's participation in the Lord's Supper might be the means for God's justifying grace to be at work. As baptized persons of all ages, we confirm God's saving act in Jesus Christ when we come together to the table. Pastors who notice un-baptized persons participating in Holy Communion should take the opportunity to talk with these persons about baptism.[6]

Our baptism invites us to share in the ministry of all Christians. When we are welcomed into the life of the church through our baptism, we begin our discipleship journey. All of us have the task of sharing the gospel. Elders and deacons, clergy of the church, remember their baptism at their ordination. Baptism was one of the pivotal events that started them on the journey toward ordained ministry.[7]

Christian marriages and Christian funerals are tied to our baptismal vows. The marriage covenant finds its foundation in the covenant between God and God's people as understood in our baptism. Pastors should remind couples during counseling sessions that the covenant they are making to one another in marriage is linked to the covenant made at their baptism. Married couples covenant to love, respect, and remain faithful to one another as reflected in God's faithfulness to each of them at their baptism. The church blesses Christian marriage based on the couple's relationship with Jesus Christ, as well as the husband's love and wife's love for each other.

Our baptism symbolizes our dying and rising to new life in Jesus Christ. When we are baptized, we begin a journey of new life in Christ and we start the journey toward our death. We are reminded each day that we must die continually to the things that keep us from putting Christ first in our lives.

In a Christian funeral we commit the deceased person to the grace and care of God. Just as in baptism we acknowledge God's covenant with us, in death we acknowledge that the deceased will enter a new covenant with God and with the saints. This individual lived in the covenant community of believers in Christ. Now he or she joins in the community of the heavenly saints. At our baptism, the pastor calls upon God's Holy Spirit to work within our lives so that we can live as faithful disciples. In our "Service of Death and Resurrection", found in *The United Methodist Hymnal*, we joyfully celebrate the life of the deceased, as we acknowledge and testify that the baptized believer faithfully embraced the baptismal call to be a true disciple of Jesus Christ.[8]

David was baptized as an infant when the waters from the baptismal font were sprinkled upon his head. Now he stands facing his congregation, taking upon himself the vows made at his baptism. He declares his own faith in Jesus as his Lord and Savior and pledges to be a faithful member of the church by his prayers, his presence, his gifts, and his service. Washed in the waters of his baptism, surrounded by a supportive community of faith, and vowing to become a faithful disciple of Jesus Christ, David continues his journey as a child of God. The journey that began at his baptism will end at his death and resurrection. Then, David will once again be cleansed with the waters of God's grace and received by a community of saints who will welcome him into the presence of God. What a journey! And it started in the church nursery!

Suggestions for Celebrating the Baptism of Infants

1. Record the baptism and give the parents the video as a gift.
2. Take pictures of the child being baptized with the pastors and scan this into the church newsletter. Share information about the baptism in the newsletter.
3. Present parents with a baptismal candle or shell, the symbol of baptism.

4. Place a picture of the baptized child and his or her family in the nursery area.

5. Have the choir sing a special anthem in honor of the child.

6. Sing a congregational hymn after the child is baptized. A suggested hymn is "Child of Blessing, Child of Promise" (*The United Methodist Hymnal*, 611).

7. Have the pastor carry the child down the aisles of the sanctuary after he or she has been baptized.

8. Let children in the congregation come forward and sit up close for the baptism of an infant.

9. Give parents a baptismal certificate.

10. Light a baptismal candle in your sanctuary each time a child is baptized.

11. Have a photographer take a picture of the child and present a framed photo to the parents.

12. Let the children of the church draw pictures of the child's baptism and present to the families.

13. Allow adopted grandparents and other persons close to the family to stand with family members at the child's baptism if parents have requested.

14. Preach sermons and teach lessons on baptism affirming the role of the congregation in fulfilling baptismal vows.

15. Have the children's committee purchase a children's book for the church library in honor of the baptized child.

16. Call the names of all children, youth, and adults baptized in the church during that year, when the church has a Renewal of Baptism service.

17. Do not ignore siblings of infants being baptized. Recognize them in the service and give them a small part such as holding the gift for the baby. Be sure and mention their names in your newsletter along with other family members.

18. Have your acolytes participate in the baptism of infants by removing the cover of the baptismal font and replacing it back after the baptism is complete.

19. Have a member of your congregation design and make a baptismal banner that can be used in the sanctuary for the baptism of a child. The children of the church might have a part in designing the banner.

20. When a single parent requests baptism, be sure and make this parent welcomed and comfortable, especially if the situation

involves an unwed mother. If family members cannot be present with the parent, arrange for a member of the children's committee, nursery committee, or your nursery coordinator to stand with the parent.

Suggestions for Helping Parents with Spiritual Formation in the Home

1. Provide brief devotional readings or Bible stories that parents can use for bedtime.
2. Provide prayers for use at mealtimes.
3. Provide suggested family activities that follow the church seasons or seasons of the year.
4. Provide family Bible readings, devotional readings, prayers, and suggested activities for Lent and Advent.
5. Give families an Advent wreath and provide brief readings to use as families light the Advent candles for the four Sundays of Advent.
6. Suggest mission projects to families.
7. Give families a list of the homebound members and encourage families to contact these persons by a card or visit.
8. Provide brief family worship litanies that can be used in the home, particularly if the family is unable to attend church due to illness.
9. Encourage families to read together the take-home curriculum sheets that their children will bring home from Sunday school.
10. Provide children with a "Lent Bag" during the season of Lent. Fill the bag with items to help teach children about the season of Lent such as: container of ashes, good-deed checklist, and prayer pretzel. For complete information about what to place in the Lent bag, consult *The Children's Minister* (Discipleship Resources). Encourage families to share the contents of the bag and talk about the meaning of the season of Lent.
11. Provide children with a Stewardship Bag to teach them about giving gifts to the church. Include in the stewardship bag a pledge card so children can pledge their time, talents, and a monetary amount to the church. Have parents share the content of the bag with their children and talk with them about the pledge card. For information on items to place in the stewardship bag, consult *The Children's Minister* (Discipleship Resources).

12. Have a library of books, videos, and resources parent can check out from the church and take home with them to learn about sharing faith with their children.
13. Encourage families to set aside one night of the week for uninterrupted meals and family conversations.
14. Encourage families to talk about faith when they are riding in the car, taking a walk, or after a sporting event. Conversations in the midst of daily living about God and faith are often more effective than scheduled devotional times.
15. Offer suggestions to families on Bibles that are appropriate for the age range of children and youth.
16. Encourage parents to subscribe to a children and youth devotional magazine and give this to their children as a gift. Recommend: *Pockets* devotional magazine for children and *DevoZine* for youth, both published by Upper Room Ministries. These are monthly devotional resources for children and youth.
17. Provide parents with *Upper Room* devotional magazine (Upper Room Ministries) for use in the home. This is a bimonthly devotional resource for adults.
18. Provide written blessings for families to use for special occasions in family life such as blessing for the first day of school, blessing for safe travel, and blessing for a new home.
19. Recommend quality religious books that parents can read to their children for bedtime or story time in the home.
20. Encourage parents to tell children their favorite Bible stories rather than always reading them from the Bible. Children enjoy hearing the stories as well as reading them from the Bible.
21. Encourage parents to ask their children questions about what they learned in Sunday school or what they heard the pastor saying in his or her sermon.
22. After worship, encourage parents to talk with their children about what was said and what happened in corporate worship.
23. Let parents know that they do not have to know all of the answers to the faith questions that children ask, but they should answer children's questions honestly, and, if they do not know an answer, turn to the church for help.
24. Provide resources for parents to talk with children on difficult issues such as death, divorce, suicide, a serious illness in the family, and other issues emerging in family life as they relate to faith.
25. Recommend Christian CDs for children and youth.

Recommended Books: Families Sharing Faith Together in the Home

Devotionals for Families

Making Time for God: Daily Devotions for Children and Families to Share, Susan R. Garrett and Amy Plantinga Pauw

As for Me and My House: 50 Easy-to-Use Devotionals for Families, Tom Zeigler and Lori Zeigler

Five Minute Devotions for Children: Celebrating God's World As a Family, Pamela Kennedy and Amy Wummer

Gather Round the Dinner Fable: Read Aloud Story Devotions For Families, Steven James

One Year Book of Family Devotions, Children's Bible Hour

A Family's Daily Devotionals for a Year: 365 Devotionals That Inspire & Bring the Family Together, Donna Coble

Prayers for Families

Together We Pray: A Prayer Book for Families, J. Bradley Wigger

Let's Say Grace: Mealtime Prayers for Family Occasions Throughout the Year, Robert M. Hamma

Unending Grace: Mealtime Prayers for Every Day of the Year, David Hauk

Bless This House: Prayers for Families and Children, Gregory Wolfe and Suzanne M. Wolfe

Thank You God for This Food: Action Prayers, Blessings and Songs for Mealtime, Debbie Trafton O'Neal and Nancy Munger

We Thank You, God, for These: Blessings and Prayers for Family Pets, Anthony F. Chiffolo and Rayner W. Hesse, Jr.

Family Activities

Gospel Games: Fun Activities for Family Home Evening and Primary, Mary H. Ross and Jennette Guymon-King

Family Fun Nights: 140 Activities the Whole Family Will Enjoy, Lisa Bany-Winters

365 Activities for Fitness, Food, and Fun For the Whole Family, Julia Sweet

Creative Family Times: Practical Activities for Building Character, Allen Hadidian and Will Wilson

The Joyful Family: Meaningful Activities and Heartfelt Celebrations for Connecting with the Ones You Love, John S. Dacey, Lynne Weygint, and Will Glennon

Activities that Teach Family Values, Tom Jackson, Frank Jackson, and Greg Bitney

Fun on the Run!: 324 Instant Family Activities, Cynthia L. Copeland

The Five Minute Parent: Fun and Fast Activities for You and Your Little Ones, Deborah Shelton

Family Fun Activity Book: Playtimes and Activities to Bring Children and Grownups Together, Bob Keeshan "Captain Kangaroo," Anne C. Cohn Connelly, and Diane Palmisciano

Chapter Seven Endnotes

1. Nagley, David & Lang, Peter. *From Font to Faith: John Wesley on Infant Baptism and the Nurture of Children* (New York: Peter Lang Publishing, Inc., 1987), 122-123.

2. Benson, Peter L. & Elkin, Carolyn H. *Effective Christian Education: A National Study of Protestant Congregations-A Summary Report on Faith, Loyalty, & Congregational Life* (Minneapolis: Search Institute, 1990), 48.

3. Ibid., 38-39.

4. Ibid., 42-44.

5. Willimon, William H. *Remember Who You Are: Baptism, A Model for Christian Life* (Nashville, The Upper Room, 1980), 71.

6. Felton, Gayle Carlton. *By Water and the Spirit: Making Connections for Identity and Ministry* (Nashville: Discipleship Resources, 2002), 43-44.

7. Ibid., 44-45.

8. Ibid., 45-47.